THE
BEER

&

FOOD

COMPANION

STEPHEN BEAUMONT

jacqui
small

*Dedicated to the memory of Michael Jackson, who charted so many
paths I have followed, including the one that led to this book.*

First published in 2015 by
Jacqui Small Llp
74-77 White Lion Street
London N1 9PF
www.jacquismallpub.com

Publisher: Jacqui Small
Senior Commissioning Editor: Fritha Saunders
Managing Editor: Emma Heyworth-Dunn
Commissioning/Project Editor: Joanna Copestick
Designer: Namkwan Cho, gradedesign.com
Recipe Photography: Peter Cassidy
Home Economist: Emily Kydd
Food Props Stylist: Iris Bromet
Picture Research: Emily Hedges
Production: Maeve Healy

British Library Cataloguing-in-Publication Data
A catalogue record for this book is available from the British Library.

10 9 8 7 6 5 4 3 2 1

ISBN 978-1-909342-99-6
Printed and bound in China

CONTENTS

FOREWORD

BY STEPHEN BEAUMONT

THIS BOOK HAS BEEN ALMOST 30 YEARS IN THE MAKING. WHEN I GREW UP, BACK IN THE 1960S AND 70S, FOOD WAS MORE ABOUT FUEL THAN IT WAS ABOUT FLAVOUR. AS KIDS, WE DIDN'T GET EXCITED ABOUT SOMETHING TRULY DELICIOUS ON OUR PLATES AS MUCH AS WE DID ABOUT PACKAGED MACARONI AND CHEESE, OR AN ENTIRE MEAL SERVED IN THE COMPARTMENTALIZED FORMAT OF A TV DINNER. FOR US, MARKETING HYPE AND NOVELTY TRUMPED TASTE 10 TIMES OUT OF 10.

It was only when I first started out as a beer writer and began to scribble notes about the beers I was trying that I began tasting new flavours in not only beer, but also in other beverages, and even in my food. Then I started to note how all those flavours went together and at that point my gastronomic life truly began. Because as much as I was relishing these new-found flavours in my food and drink – the surprising sweetness of fresh lemon juice, the oddly appealing metallic tang of blood in a slice of rare steak, the floral notes in a saaz-hopped pilsner – I was even more fascinated when two tastes thrown together at the table combined to create a flavour experience that was gloriously greater than the sum of their parts. For my young palate, this was alchemy of the most marvellous kind.

A few years later, while in Vancouver beginning research on my first book, the *Great Canadian Beer Guide*, I hosted my debut beer and food tasting event featuring beer and chocolate pairings. Even though the beers were

of indisputable pedigree (vintage Thomas Hardy's Ale and Swiss-brewed Samichlaus among them), with chocolates from a noted local chocolatier, as I surveyed the room just prior to beginning my talk, I saw little other than scepticism reflected back at me.

Undeterred, I charged boldly ahead through that series of eight pairings, finding that after two or three, disbelief began to be replaced by surprise, and doubt turned to joy, so that by the end of it all, we were a roomful of very happy converts to the church of beer and chocolate. Over the next two years, I repeated these tastings at every opportunity, sometimes with chocolate, at other times with cheese and occasionally in the form of a beer dinner, which was still quite unusual at the time. All of which led to the development of my second book, *A Taste for Beer*.

Beer and food pairing has mushroomed in popularity in recent years, to the point that we now have entire restaurants devoted to the practice. This book celebrates the optimization of the enjoyment of eating and drinking food and beer. It's not a 'pinky-finger-in-the-air' beer and food pairing, or a snobbish declaration of what beer really must be served with this or that other high-end dish, but simply an explanation of why certain pairings work and why others don't.

As I have asked so often during the 20 years I've been matching beer with food, when you have the chance to take two great flavours and put them together in such a way that the resulting taste is better than that of either component part, why on earth would you choose not to do so?

Cheers!
Stephen Beaumont

INTRODUCTION

INTRODUCTION

A SHORT HISTORY OF BEER AND FOOD

WHEN A GROUP OF DINERS SIT DOWN AT THE TABLE AFTER HAVING ENJOYED A RANGE OF PRE-DINNER DRINKS – A MARTINI HERE AND A GLASS OF CHABLIS OR A PILSNER THERE – THE ANSWER TO THE QUESTION ABOUT WHAT TO DRINK WITH THE MEAL IS, USUALLY, WINE.

Many people may not know why they are ordering wine, but they will most likely be united in the belief that it is the right and proper thing to do.

Wine is often chosen despite the fact that a single bottle does not divide generously into six glasses, since, at a mere 125ml (4fl oz) apiece per person, it means a second bottle will need to be ordered almost immediately. Sometimes wine is chosen despite the differing pairing needs of a diverse food order featuring beef prominently on one plate, vegetables on another and fish on a third. And it will often be wine despite the high tariffs placed on it by restaurants. But, most of all, it's wine because of a quirk of history.

For the majority of the western world, certainly the English-speaking portion of it, gastronomy was learned from the French. It was they who formalized meal service in the 18th century – dinner *à la française*, as noted by Margaret Visser in her landmark book, *The Rituals of Dinner* – and it was they who later lent us the word we use to describe the 'programme' or 'menu', outlining the meal to follow. Even today, a lot of our food terminology is French, from *hors d'oeuvre* to *serviette* to the main-event dish, the *pièce de resistance*.

When restaurant culture began to integrate itself into modern Anglophone society, we took our cues from the French: we adopted the aperitif as a pre-dinner drink, laid our tables in the French fashion, with a multiplicity of knives and forks and spoons, and our grand restaurants prided themselves on offering 'French service'. And of course we drank wine with our meals.

We drank wine because the French drank wine, and the French drank, and continue to drink, wine because they live in a wine-producing country. Not because wine necessarily pairs with food better than beer does, but because wine was

firmly established as France's beverage of choice, so it became our mealtime favourite too.

Had Anglophone dining habits originated somewhere other than France, things might be much different today. Again from Visser's *The Rituals of Dinner*:

'WINE AND BEER CAN SUPPORT POWERFUL SOCIAL ROLES… BECAUSE PEOPLE HAVE CHOSEN THEM TO DO SO. THESE DRINKS, IN EUROPE, ACCOMPANY FOOD BECAUSE THEY ARE FERMENTED RATHER THAN DISTILLED, AND ARE CONSIDERED NUTRITIOUS AND HEALTHFUL, LIKE DINNER ITSELF. THEY THEN SEEM MORE INNOCUOUS THAN OTHER LIQUORS BECAUSE THEY ARE CONSUMED AT THE TABLE.'

Note the joining of wine and beer as two sides of the same fermented coin. Had modern western gastronomy found its roots in Bavaria, England, the Czech Republic or even French Alsace, rather than in Parisian dining rooms and central France, we might have been dining with pilsners and märzens, or pale ales and porters, rather than with the wines of Bordeaux and Burgundy.

OPPOSITE ABOVE The British pub is one of the many places where beer and food have been enjoyed together for hundreds of years.

OPPOSITE BELOW The choice of beers that work well with food has never been so wide as now, at the start of the 21st century. Whether you prefer light ale or dark stout, there is a beer for every type of food.

Since its discovery, alcohol has been prized among most humans. We celebrate with it and mourn with it, we serve it at huge parties and share it with loved ones on the most intimate of occasions; we treat it as a social elixir and view it also as an important component of our meals. When it is taken away from us, as it was during the wrongheaded experiment known as Prohibition, we will go to great lengths to get it anyway.

And of all the alcoholic beverages we know today, beer is most likely the oldest. Archaeologists have determined it to be at least 10,000 years old, and possibly much older, and while we don't know for certain when the very first beer was brewed, we do know that it probably found its first home in Sumer.

Popularly known as the 'cradle of civilisation', ancient Sumer existed in the fertile area between the Tigris and Euphrates rivers, near the Persian Gulf. It was there that historians believe mankind ceased to be nomadic, instead settling into communities and farming for subsistence. And the reason may have been beer.

The theory goes that one reason the Sumerians decided to cease their wandering was so they could plant and grow fields of grain, which was an important nutrient and, of course, the principle ingredient in beer. In fact, the production of grain for beer could possibly have been the primary reason for the Sumerian farming tradition, so important is the beverage thought to have been to them.

By the time of ancient Egypt, brewing had become big business, with commercial operations turning out beer that was sold up and down the River Nile, wars waged with funds accrued from the sale of beer and workers paid for their labours in, you guessed it, beer. Beer style had even become a factor, with multiple varieties being made and a strict hierarchy of who was allowed to consume each type – with the best always reserved for the Pharaohs and their families, often served at lavish feasts.

Brewing became such a skilled industry in Egypt that even the Romans were impressed, noting in the 1st century BC that the Egyptians made 'a drink of barley... for smell and sweetness of taste it is not much inferior to wine'. High praise indeed from wine drinkers.

For the next couple of millennia, beer continued to perform important functions in daily life, from foodstuff – as far back as the Sumerians and Egyptians, beer was thought of as 'liquid bread' and prized for its nutrition as much as for its intoxicating effects – to social elixir and ceremonial cornerstone. For most of that time, its production was confined to monasteries and farmhouses, the former being the first commercial brewing operations in the modern world, until eventually the business trade caught on and the notion of an inn was developed, where a voyager could find a bed and sustenance, and beer, for a fixed price.

The arrival of the inn was an important one in northern beer-drinking nations, since a brewery was considered a

LEFT An Eighteenth Dynasty painting on an Egyptian memorial stone shows a Syrian mercenary drinking beer in the company of his Egyptian wife and child.

OPPOSITE A 1630 painting by Pieter Brueghel the Younger is entitled *Peasants Merrymaking Outside the Swan Inn in a Village Street*.

vital piece of any such operation. (Prior to the inn, travellers had the choice of bedding down in a comfortable-looking field or seeking shelter at a monastery, usually one with a brewery.) And so began the spread of commercial brewing in Europe and, eventually, around the globe, with food and hospitality as close companions the whole way.

Over time that began to change, at least in parts of the world, with beer drinking becoming increasingly separate from eating, even to the point that publicans and bar owners began to view their food offerings as an afterthought, if indeed they even bothered with food at all. In North America, Prohibition sealed the deal and when beer finally returned to the social milieu, it was as a drink, pure and simple. In the United Kingdom around the same time, pub food embarked upon a slow but seemingly inexorable decline, to the point that it eventually became a bit of a global joke.

Thankfully, the rise of craft beer and the corresponding spread of the 'gastropub' concept – which, however despised the word might now have become, is unquestionably responsible for a dramatic improvement in the quality of pub and bar food since the early 1990s – have combined to swing the pendulum back to the point that beer once again has assumed its rightful place at the table. And not just alongside pizza or chicken wings or a big plate of fish and chips either, but also with steak frites, paella, sushi and anything else the great and global world of gastronomy would care to offer.

Indeed, today even wine-drinking nations like Italy and France are embracing the new world of beer, to the point that bottles of ale and lager are replacing Chiantis and sauvignon blancs at many a Roman or Parisian dinner table. Beer is back, and that is definitely something to celebrate, with terrific brews matched to delectable plates of simple, fine or formal fare.

THE ESSENCE OF BEER

THE ESSENCE OF BEER

INGREDIENTS AND INFINITE FLAVOURS

AT ITS HEART, BEER IS A PRETTY SIMPLE BEVERAGE: STEEP SOME GERMINATED GRAIN IN WARM WATER; DRAIN OFF THE LIQUID AND BOIL IT WITH SOME HOPS; DRAIN THAT OFF, LET IT COOL DOWN AND ADD SOME YEAST; WAIT A FEW DAYS AND – VOILA – YOU HAVE BEER.

WATER, BARLEY MALT, YEAST AND HOPS

This simplicity, however, belies the complex alchemy that produces the beverage so many of us take for granted. Because beyond that simple equation of grain + water + hops + yeast = beer, there are any number of decisions that need to be made, each and every one of which can dramatically change the flavour and character of the finished beer.

The use of greater amounts of grain, for instance, will result in more sugar in the unfermented beer, or wort, which in turn will most likely lead to a stronger finished beer. Add more hops at the start of the boil and the beer will be more bitter; throw them in at the end and it will emerge more aromatically charged. Ferment the lot at cooler temperatures with the proper yeast strain and you'll have a lager, whereas a different yeast at warmer temperatures will produce an ale. And those are but three of the more fundamental decisions a brewer needs to make.

Will the beer be *Reinheitsgebot* pure, which is to say brewed from only malted grain, hops, barley and yeast? Should spices be added at some point in the process, or maybe extra sugar for fermentation? Do you want the hops to add citrussy flavours or notes of tropical fruit or spicy nuttiness? Will it be dark or light, richly malty or thinner and hoppier? Filtered or unfiltered or bottle conditioned? The list goes on and on.

All of this leaves the average beer drinker grasping for some idea of what to expect from a beer that often offers scant information on its label, if indeed it even has a label. Beer styles help, of course, but only to the degree that brewers are willing to follow them. (And, as we will find a bit later on, that's a fairly big variable). Method is all important, too, from the mix of grains used, to the temperature at which the beer is fermented and then conditioned, but no one should need to take a degree in brewing science in order to be able to choose their style of beer wisely.

Let's start with the basic ingredients, and the most abundant one at that, water.

OPPOSITE The bad boys of British beer, the minds behind Brewdog have taken beer styles, as well as marketing, to new and sometimes audacious levels.

RIGHT The use of self-adhesive labels, often applied by hand rather than by machine, allow breweries like North Cornwall's Harbour Brewing to produce bottled beer with less equipment and expense than otherwise might be the case.

Between 90 and 96 per cent of any beer you drink is water, but I'll bet that you've never given its composition much of a second thought. Don't feel bad; very few of us do.

WATER IS BOTH THE MOST AND LEAST IMPORTANT PART OF A BEER. AS A PRINCIPLE, INDEED PRIMARY, COMPONENT OF EACH AND EVERY SIP, LOGIC DICTATES THAT IT MUST PLAY A MAJOR ROLE IN A BEER'S BASIC CHARACTER.

Yet because water is by its nature a relatively neutral taste, the impact it has on the overall flavour as discerned by the average beer drinker can be considered minor.

For the brewer, however, water composition is key. So much so, in fact, that entire brewing texts have been devoted to the subject.

What it all boils down to is mineral composition. Although the basic nomenclature of water accurately defines it as two molecules of hydrogen to every molecule of oxygen, the environment from which we draw our water – springs in the earth or treatment plants in the city – will also have a strong effect on its structure and taste. This, in turn, will influence how suited it may be to different styles of beer.

While brewers today can adjust their water profiles with relative ease, this was obviously not always the case, which is why in centuries past breweries tended to cluster around large sources of spring water. One such famous 'cluster' was

in the English Midlands brewing town of Burton-on-Trent, which is considered to be the birthplace of pale ale.

It was a confluence of a number of factors that cemented Burton's place in brewing history, but the water it provided – and continues to provide – to brewers figures highly among them. Wealthy in mineral salts, Burton's underground spring water was ideally suited to the ales that were then being produced by English brewers, to the point that it once boasted dozens of breweries, despite a population that comprised only several thousand. Such was the respect once accorded Burton ale that even today certain breweries are known to 'Burtonize' their brewing water, which is to say they add mineral salts to it, such as calcium and magnesium sulphates. It is a water profile considered by many to be ideal for pale ales and IPAs.

Conversely, the gentle, floral flavours of Bohemian hops such as the famed Saaz are reflected in the soft waters of that Czech region, combining to create the delicate and fragrant Czech style of pilsner. Thus brewers around the world seeking to emulate that particular approach to lager will often de-mineralize their brewing water.

To the beer drinker, however, these aqua-manipulations are definitely of secondary interest. Far more pivotal are a beer's other primary ingredients.

OPPOSITE The composition of water locally available to a brewery was once key to providing a unique flavour for its beer. Nowadays brewers are capable of altering a water profile using purely scientific techniques.

BELOW The Purity Brewing Co. in Warwickshire, England recycles it water on the wetlands adjacent to its farm-based brewery.

BARLEY MALT is the basic building block of beer in that it provides sugar for fermentation, but before it can be used, it must first be malted. In a nutshell, malting is the procedure by which starches – simple sugars – are released from the grain. The process involves steeping the barley in water until it sprouts, which is essentially the same process as placing an avocado stone in a jar of water and watching it germinate. Unlike the avocado experiment, however, maltsters do not want the grain to spawn a plant, so they halt its growth cycle by lightly cooking, or kilning, immediately after sprouting so that it's ready for brewing.

It is what happens after germination is arrested that really affects the flavour of a beer. After the basic kiln, what's left is pale barley malt, which forms the base of most ordinary blonde lagers and is the base malt for most beers, regardless of hue. It's used to provide fermentable sugars and a bit of grainy flavour. Known as 'two-row' for the way it grows on the barley stalk, it is used mainly for its fermentable sugars and slightly grainy flavour, and is what you will find in the large-to-massive silos that are essential equipment at all but the smallest breweries.

Once the pale malt is made, maltsters will continue with the toasting to create what are known as speciality malts. These grains range from faintly coloured – barely toasted bread as opposed to a fresh slice – to tan and faintly caramelized, all the way to deep black and roasty. And what they supply to a beer is far more than fermentable sugars.

When a light amber lager or ale includes toffee flavours or cooked sugar, it's all down to caramelized malts. If coffee flavours are found in your porter or stout, that will be the work of black malts and roasted barley, the latter of which is sometimes added unmalted, for flavour. If your beer tastes smoky, it's likely to have been made with a speciality malt that is not kilned over an indirect heat source, as most malts are, but dried and smoked over a wood fire.

In addition to these flavours and numerous others, barley malt is also responsible for 100 per cent of the colour of beer, unless there is added fruit or caramel. Colour has nothing to do with the strength or calorie content of the beer, both of which are largely determined by the amount of sugar made available for fermentation. Most of barley malt's flavour influence arises when it partners with yeast.

YEAST makes alcohol. It really is as simple as that; remove yeast from the equation and fermentation does not take place. Throughout the history of brewing it was not known what made fermentation happen, only that it happened. Bavarian brewers used to skim off what they called '*Gött ist gut*', or 'God is good', from their fermenting beer because they knew it would cause further fermentation in the next batch, but they really didn't know why. Brewers in ancient times were likely to have drawn the same empirical conclusions.

In 1876, Louis Pasteur finally isolated yeast and sorted it from the other micro-organisms that could spoil the taste of beer. The resulting realization was that there were two main families of yeast in brewing, each imparting generalized flavour traits to the beer.

ABOVE LEFT Barley provides a beer with sugar for fermentation once it has been malted and germination halted at the right time.

OPPOSITE During fermentation, yeast expels not only alcohol, but also the carbonation that is elemental to all but a handful of beer styles.

The general genus of brewing yeasts is Saccharomyces. There are several types, but only two important ones for brewers: *Saccharomyces cerevisiae* and *Saccharomyces pastorianus*. The former is ale yeast, referred to as warm-fermenting or top-fermenting yeast because it does most of its work near the top of the fermenter and functions best at warmer temperatures, while the latter, lager yeast, is also known as bottom-fermenting or cool-fermenting yeast.

Ale yeasts work at warmer temperatures and tend to produce esters or fruity flavours, whereas lager yeasts tend not to, or do so to a much smaller degree. Such flavours, regardless of whether they are easily perceived as berry, peach or other fruity notes or indeed barely perceived at all, often give the beer a fuller, richer mouthfeel and character.

Yeasts interact with sugars produced by the barley malt in many different ways, creating not just alcohol and carbon dioxide, but also a vast diversity of flavours. While these different tastes are far too varied to itemize, it is worth noting that the most easily recognized yeast-derived by-products of banana and clove aromas and flavours, come from a family of yeasts used in German-style wheat beers.

Beyond *S. cerevisiae* and *S. pastorianus*, modern brewers make use of a number of other yeasts and assorted microflora in order to flavour their beers, most notoriously Brettanomyces, which delivers appealing earthy, musty and sometimes barnyard-ish aromas and flavours. (Brett, as the yeast is known for short, is thought by many to create mainly tart flavours, but in fact such tastes arise instead from bacteria often employed in conjunction with Brett, such as Pediococcus and Lactobacillus). These beers are products of spontaneous fermentation, while modern examples, with cultured, controlled versions of wild yeasts and bacteria, are the result of mixed fermentation.

All beers that exhibit the effects of Brettanomyces, Pediococcus and other such yeasts and bacteria have become known as 'sour beers', although a more accurate descriptor might be tart, the two flavours being subtly different. Rather like the taste of freshly squeezed lemon juice (tart) as compared to the juice of a shrivelled lemon that has been sitting in the fridge for a few weeks (sour).

As much as yeast and grain sugars conspire to create a vast number of flavours and aromas in beer, their contribution is often overshadowed by that of a plant about which many beer drinkers know nothing. I refer to the spice of beer, the diminutive pine cone-shaped flowers of the vine *Humulus lupulus*, better known as hops.

Originally introduced to beer as a preservative, hops are grown on vines so voracious that they can reach upwards of 6m (19ft 6in) in height over the course of a single season, growing up to 30cm (1ft) per day. When mature, they are harvested and dried, so as to keep viable the essential active ingredient, a yellow powder known as lupulin contained within the cone. Most often the cones are pelletized and vacuum sealed for freshness, although sometimes they are packaged as whole hops. Storage is best under refrigeration.

Occasionally hops are employed in their fresh, undried state for a class of beers known generally as 'wet hop' or 'fresh hop' beers, which are usually ales and most often fall broadly into the pale ale or India pale ale style.

In the brewhouse hops are added to the wort during its boiling stage, with those added earlier on in the boil contributing more bitterness and those added during the latter stages being primarily for aromatic purposes. Sometimes more aroma hops are added during the post-fermentation maturation process, known as conditioning, in a practice called dry-hopping.

USED IN MODERATION, HOPS PROVIDE A DRYING BITTERNESS THAT CAN MAKE EVEN A NOTICEABLY GRAINY LAGER SEEM QUITE QUENCHING. MORE FREQUENTLY OF LATE, HOWEVER, HOPS ARE BEING USED IN RELATIVE ABUNDANCE TO CREATE ROBUST BITTERNESS, SOMETIMES WITH AND SOMETIMES WITHOUT A SOLID AND MALTY BACKBONE OF FLAVOUR FOR SUPPORT. THIS PRACTICE BRINGS TO THE FORE THE FUNDAMENTAL FLAVOUR CHARACTERISTICS OF VARIOUS HOP VARIETIES.

Without delving into every single variety of hops in existence, it is enough to mention here a few of the main tastes which arise from different hops. For example, generally speaking, hops grown in the principle and traditional regions of Europe – Kent in England, Hallertau in Germany, Saaz in the Czech Republic – tend towards more moderate, even restrained aromas and flavours, such as floral notes, spiciness or nuttiness. New World hops, on the other hand, such as the American-grown 'C-hops' – Cascade, Centennial, Chinook and Citra, among others – offer bold flavours and aromas of citrus, passion fruit and even pine resin.

Newer still are New Zealand-grown hops like Motueka and Nelson Sauvin, and Australian-grown Galaxy, which deliver particular flavours of tropical fruit. Even more recently a German hop-cultivation project has yielded new and surprisingly fruity hops such as the aptly-named Mandarina Bavaria. More varieties with ever more diverse flavour and aroma characteristics will surely follow.

LEFT Originally used as a preservative in beer, hops now vary tremendously, from the restrained aromas of the British Kent hop fields to the bold, citrus flavours of the American C-hops and the tropical fruit flavours of New World hops.

While many brewers, German and otherwise, still adhere religiously to the standard set out by the *Reinheitsgebot*, the Bavarian purity law that limits ingredients to malted grain, hops, water and yeast, the majority of the world's modern day brewers are unhampered by such restraints. This can lead to some interesting brewing ingredients.

More conventional additions include different grains, such as wheat, rye and oats, as well as such non-glutinous grains like buckwheat, sorghum and others for a new wave of gluten-free beers. Of the first three, wheat is by far the most popular, featuring in such established beer styles as weissbier (German-style wheat beer), Belgian-style wheat or white beer (or witbier or bière blanche) and American wheat ale, the last including everything from softly flavourful golden ales to potent wheat wines. Rye is experiencing a current revival, after having been ignored by brewers for decades, and features most often in rye pale ales and 'RyePAs', or IPAs made from a portion of malted rye. Oats are traditionally found in oatmeal stouts, where they add a silkiness to the beer, but may now also be found in brown ales and other sorts of beer.

BEFORE WE BEGAN THE ERA OF HOPPED BEER, IN OTHER WORDS FOR ABOUT 90 PER CENT OF BEER'S KNOWN HISTORY, ALES WERE FLAVOURED WITH ALL MANNER OF FRUITS AND HERBS AND SPICES, FROM JUNIPER BERRIES TO CORIANDER SEEDS, HEATHER TO BOG MYRTLE. SO IT SHOULDN'T COME AS A SURPRISE THAT BREWERS TODAY ARE FLAVOURING THEIR BREWS WITH THESE SAME INGREDIENTS, AND OFTEN MANY OTHERS BESIDES.

Broadly, fruit beers form their own category, but they also vary widely. Belgian lambic brewers, for example, will re-ferment their spontaneously-fermented wheat beers with whole cherries, raspberries and other fruits, producing finished beers that are fermented dry, but still bear the colour, aroma and flavour of the fruits used. Other brewers will simply add fruit juices or extracts to their fully fermented and conditioned beers, creating sweet and strongly fruity beers, while others still will employ fruit flavourings in harmony with non-fermentable sweeteners. The style of the base beer can also range dramatically, from the common light wheat beer to stouts and porters or even strong barley wines aged in barrels with fruit.

Spiced beers offer similar diversity, from the coriander and dried bitter orange peel considered essential to a Belgian-style wheat beer to beers heavily seasoned with a kitchen cabinet-worth of herbs and spices. Sometimes the spices almost completely define the beer's character, while in other beers a judiciously employed flavouring can add a subtly altering top-note to an otherwise well-defined taste profile.

Today's brewers being the adventurous, iconoclastic lot that they are, it is hard to imagine an ingredient that they have not at some point added to a beer. Tobacco leaf? Yes, although the result was not to be commended. Carrot beer? From the now-defunct Kitchen Brewery in England. Kumquat IPA? Absolutely, and Dieu du Ciel's Disco Soleil from Canada is actually shockingly good. Doughnut toppings? Thanks to a series of beers Rogue Ales has produced in conjunction with Oregon's Voodoo Doughnut chain, yes, even that.

ABOVE Rye, oates, fruits and spices have all been used over the years to add additional flavour to beer. Currently there is a big revival in the use of interesting adjuncts in many craft breweries around the world.

BEER STYLES

BEER STYLES

HOW DO WE MAKE SENSE OF ALL THIS?

WHEN MICHAEL JACKSON CHRONICLED THE WORLD OF BEER IN TERMS OF STYLE IN HIS 1977 BOOK, *THE WORLD GUIDE TO BEER*, AN EFFORT WIDELY VIEWED TODAY AS THE FIRST ATTEMPT TO DO SO, HE OUTLINED 24 SUCH STYLES, NOT INCLUDING THE GENERAL, OVER-ARCHING TERMS 'LAGER' AND 'ALE'.

When 222 judges gathered in Denver, Colorado in October 2014, to adjudicate American ales and lagers in the Great American Beer Festival Competition, they did so in 90 categories. While that might seem an impressively large number, the Brewers Association, which oversees the GABF Competition, itself recognizes over 50 further categories, so a grand total of 141 global beer styles – almost six times the number identified by Jackson.

WHILE THIS EXPLOSION OF BEER STYLES IS AT LEAST PARTIALLY UNDERSTANDABLE GIVEN THE CORRESPONDING GROWTH OF CRAFT BREWING WORLDWIDE OVER THE LAST 30–40 YEARS, THE OBSESSIVE NEED TO CATEGORIZE EVERY BEER IN THE WORLD BY STYLE HAS ACTUALLY BEGUN TO HAVE THE OPPOSITE EFFECT FOR WHICH BEER STYLES WERE ORIGINALLY INTENDED. INSTEAD OF INFORMING, THEY ARE CONFOUNDING.

Return for a moment to Michael Jackson's seminal book. Written during a period when beer was decidedly more national or even regional than it was global, Jackson's goal in defining styles was to present a guide for consumers so that they might, for example, understand that a traditional Belgian lambic beer would present a very different drinking experience than would a British best bitter or German märzen. And it worked.

Today, however, beer style has bled into beer marketing, so that the manner in which a beer is described has as much to do with how it tastes as it does with what is presently hot in the marketplace. Hence the 2014–2015 proliferation of IPA variants, which may now be said to include black, white and red interpretations, as well as Belgian and lagered versions, in potencies ranging from 3.5% ABV to two, three or four times that strength. There are even IPAs born of a mixed fermentation featuring Brettanomyces and other undomesticated yeasts.

In case you missed the phenomenon, the India pale ale, or IPA, soared from the fringes to become, over a period of only a few years, by far the most popular and bestselling craft beer style in North America and, increasingly, the world. The end result being the 'every beer is an IPA' movement.

All of this may leave the beer drinker wondering if the notion of 'beer style' even has meaning any more. And to be frank, in a world where a single style can have so many dramatic variances; traditionally low-alcohol styles can be 'Imperialized' to many times their typical strength; and even the most apparently straightforward style can easily wind up dosed with herbs or fruits, aged in bourbon barrels or amped up with truckloads of hops, this is a legitimate concern.

Yet for all this obfuscation, styles must still have an uncontestable place in the world of beer, and even more so in a book like this. How else can you be directed to a suitable beer for a specific dish if not by style? And when shopping for a refreshing lager for summer or a soothing ale for winter, surely style is the only way to be sure of an unfamiliar brew being well suited to the occasion?

What I propose, then, is a simplified approach to beer styles, defined first by general flavour traits – bitter or sweet, light or robust – and then by an over-arching category. Each of these categories I have then broken down into common styles and fringe styles, the latter of which exist primarily to capitalize on the popularity of one or more of the established styles.

BITTER, HOP-FORWARD ALES

BOLD

IT IS OFTEN SAID THAT BITTERNESS IS A LEARNED OR 'ADULT' TASTE, BUT YOU WOULDN'T KNOW IT FROM THE POPULARITY OF THESE SOMETIMES BRAWNY BRUISERS. BITTERNESS HERE CAN RANGE FROM DRYING NUTTINESS ALL THE WAY TO FORCEFUL GRAPEFRUIT OR PINY FLAVOURS.

PALE ALE/BEST BITTER/ INDIA PALE ALE

This collection of ales is defined principally by hop content, beginning with a dry and mild to moderate bitterness and progressing through to intensely bitter. Seldom do these beers show strong maltiness or sweetness, although fruity esters are commonplace and, in fact, serve well to provide a base for the bitterness of the beer.

COMMON STYLES

- **TRADITIONAL PALE ALE/BEST BITTER:** Biscuity or dryly caramel malt, balanced with nutty or spicy hops.
- **BLONDE/GOLDEN BITTER:** As above, but with a paler hue and often gentle fruitiness.
- **AMERICAN-STYLE PALE ALE:** Pale malt with strongly citrussy or resinous hoppiness.
- **TRADITIONAL INDIA PALE ALE (IPA):** Usually like the British-style pale ale, but stronger and hoppier, though sometimes close to identical. Occasionally quite low-strength versions are also found in the UK.
- **AMERICAN-STYLE INDIA PALE ALE (IPA):** Almost always stronger, at 7% ABV or greater, and very much hoppier than the American-style pale ale.
- **DOUBLE OR IMPERIAL IPA:** Very high strength IPAs, stretching to as much as 10% ABV or more, and occasionally similar to an American-style barley wine.

FRINGE STYLES

Black IPA (hoppy porter); White IPA (hoppy Belgian-style wheat beer); Red IPA (hoppy amber ale); Belgian IPA (IPA fermented with a variety of yeast that yields spicy or funky aromas and flavours); Triple IPA (very strong double IPA); session IPA (low-alcohol IPA, usually below 5% ABV).

KEY BEERS

1. Traditional pale ale/Best bitter: **MARSTON'S PEDIGREE, FULLER'S ESB**

2. Blonde/Golden bitter: **HOPBACK SUMMER LIGHTNING, CELT GOLDEN AGE**

3. American-style pale ale: **SIERRA NEVADA PALE ALE**

4. Traditional India pale ale (IPA): **THORNBRIDGE JAIPUR, BURTON BRIDGE EMPIRE INDIA PALE ALE**

5. American-style India pale ale (IPA): **ANCHOR LIBERTY ALE, FOUNDERS CENTENNIAL IPA**

6. Double or Imperial IPA: **RUSSIAN RIVER PLINY THE ELDER**

SAISON

Originating as a farmhouse beer brewed at the end of the spring brewing season to be stored for drinking over summer, the saison style has in modern days become a bit of a dumping ground for all sorts of moderately strong ales fermented with one of a handful of yeasts of Belgian origin.

COMMON STYLE

- **SAISON**: Usually light to medium gold in colour, with a slighty to moderately spicy character and moderate hop bitterness, ideally finishing quite dryly.

FRINGE STYLE

Saison (A rare instance where the fringe style is the same as the proper style, in this case comprising a diversity of beers labelled 'saison' that may be heavily spiced, sweet in character or otherwise quite dissimilar to the original beer).

KEY BEERS

1. **SAISON DUPONT**
2. **BRASSERIE DE JANDRAIN-JANDRENOUILLE IV SAISON**

DRYLY BITTER LAGERS

CRISP

COOL FERMENTATION'S ANSWER TO 'BOLD' STYLE ALES, THESE ARE SOME OF THE BEER WORLD'S MOST REFRESHING BEERS, WITH LEAN, QUENCHING MALTINESS AND A HOP CHARACTER THAT, WHILE IT CAN EASILY STRAY TO THE BITTER, MOST OFTEN EMPHASIZES THE DRYING NATURE OF THE NOBLE HOP.

PILSNER

This group of lagers represents the vast majority of the volume of beer consumed around the world, since such global best-sellers as Budweiser, Heineken and the Chinese beer Snow are all technically of the pilsner style. What separates those brews from the more literal offspring of the original pilsner, Pilsner Urquell, however, is hoppiness, which will be found in varying degrees in all proper pilsners.

COMMON STYLE

- **CZECH- OR BOHEMIAN-STYLE PILSNER:** Usually medium-bodied lagers with light to medium maltiness contributing caramel notes of corresponding depth and weight, plus a typical Saaz hop aroma and flavour giving the fresh beer a floral and moderately bitter character.
- **GERMAN-STYLE PILSNER:** Generally light bodied and moderately to well-hopped, resulting in a strong perception of bitterness.
- **GLOBAL-STYLE PILSNER:** Mass-market lagers with only a passing similarity to the pilsner styles noted above, pale and rarely anything more than lightly bitter.

FRINGE STYLES

Imperial pilsner : strong pilsner, usually of 8% ABV or higher); Imperial pale lager (an IPA derivative; like the Imperial pilsner, but usually with a stronger hoppiness).

KEY BEERS

1. Czech or Bohemian-style pilsner: **PILSNER URQUELL, BUDVAR/CZECHVAR**
2. German-style pilsner: **JEVER, SQUATTERS PIVO PILSNER**
3. Global style pilsner: **SAGRES, CRUZCAMPO, PERONI**

THE DEFINING CHARACTER OF THESE BEERS MIGHT BE SAID TO BE 'BALANCE'. NOT TOO BITTER, NOT TOO SWEET, MILDLY FRUITY AT BEST AND SELDOM OVERLY ASSERTIVE, EVEN WHEN THEY OCCASIONALLY CLIMB UP THE STRENGTH LADDER, THEY ARE BEERS WELL SUITED TO THE FINE ART OF CONVERSATION.

GOLDEN ALE

A general catch-all category that includes a variety of ales broadly styled to appeal to pilsner drinkers. Arguably the original is kölsch, a beer native to the German city of Köln (Cologne) while derivatives include a broad swathe of ales variously described as blonde or golden.

COMMON STYLE

- **KÖLSCH:** The product of warm fermentation coupled with long, cold lagering, producing a light-hued beer with subdued to non-existent fruitiness, a subtly rounded body and a light to moderate bitterness.

- **GOLDEN/BLONDE ALE:** Mostly New World beers originally designed to attract lager drinkers to the craft beer fold, but now often quite interesting, subtly complex ales with soft fruitiness and drying hoppiness.

- **BELGIAN-STYLE ENKEL OR SINGLE ALE:** Originally the lower strength beer enjoyed every day by monks, modern versions tend to be mildly caramel sweet and slightly to notably spicy in flavour, although spices are typically not employed during brewing.

- **BELGIAN-STYLE TRIPEL:** Developed at Belgium's Westmalle monastery brewery in the early 1930s, combining pale malt with high strength, fruity

maltiness and drying and moderately bittering hoppiness.

- **CREAM ALE/STEAM BEER:** Beers of hybrid fermentation – the former with an ale yeast and lager conditioning, the latter with a lager yeast fermented at warmer temperatures – and American in origin. Steam beer is generally viewed as the more complex of the two and can boast significant hoppiness to go along with its biscuit maltiness, while most modern cream ales are blonde, gently sweet and often grainy. (Since the term 'steam beer' is copyrighted by the Anchor Brewing Company of San Francisco, California, such beers are often marketed as California common beers.)

KEY BEERS

1. Kölsch: **GAFFEL KÖLSCH, MALZMÜHLE MÜHLEN KÖLSCH**
2. Golden/Blonde ale: **TOWNSITE BREWING ZUNGA, YRIA GOLDEN**
3. Belgian-style enkel or single ale: **CHIMAY GOLD**
4. Belgian-style tripel: **WESTMALLE TRIPEL, NEW HOLLAND BLACK TULIP TRIPEL**
5. Cream ale/Steam beer: **ANCHOR STEAM BEER, SLEEMAN CREAM ALE**

PALE LAGER

The popularity of pale malt after the development of the first pilsner in 1867 led to changes in many beer styles, but none more fundamental than the shift in Bavaria from dunkel lagers to helles, or pale lagers.

COMMON STYLES

- **HELLES:** The modern default beer style of Bavaria, helles beers are of moderate strength, usually 4.5% to 5% ABV, with a gentle malty sweetness and a crisp, dry finish.
- **MÄRZEN/OKTOBERFESTBIER:** Synonymous styles with traditional and modern interpretations, old-style märzen being deep gold to light amber with flavours that lean from toasted malt to slightly roasty and modern interpretations that are more honey-ish, sweet and bright gold in colour. Both are generally slightly strong at +/- 6% ABV.
- **VIENNA LAGER:** Deep gold to light amber lagers of moderate strength, with gentle, sometimes toasty or roasty sweetness in the body and a dry finish.

KEY BEERS

1. Helles: **AUGUSTINER LAGERBIER HELL, STEAM WHISTLE PILSNER**
2. Märzen/Oktoberfestbier: **HOFBRÄU OKTOBERFESTBIER, REAL ALE OKTOBERFEST**
3. Vienna Lager: **KING VIENNA LAGER, MINERVA VIENA**

DARK & SWEET, MALT LED BEERS

MELLOW

FOR THOSE WHO DESIRE A BIT MORE TO THEIR BEERS THAN MERE SOCIABILITY, THESE ARE WELL-STRUCTURED ALES AND LAGERS WITH A BIT MORE CHARACTER THAN THEIR LIGHTER-HUED KIN. OFTEN A BIT NUTTY OR ROASTY, THEY ARE DEFINED BY THE DARKER MALTS THAT HELP FORM THEIR BACKBONE FLAVOURS.

MILD ALE

Although the term 'mild' was originally employed in England to denote a youthful ale fresh from the brewery, in modern parlance it refers to a low-alcohol ale, usually, but not necessarily, dark in colour.

COMMON STYLE

*   **MILD:** Low in strength – usually +/- 3.5% ABV – and slightly sweet and malty, often with light, roasted-malt flavours and sometimes with a soft, hop bitterness.

FRINGE STYLE

Imperial mild: while there is historical precedence for high-alcohol mild ales in the sense that 'mild' once meant brewery fresh, many brewers today make 'Imperial mild' as an ironic reference to the modern, low-strength definition.

KEY BEERS

1. **MOORHOUSE'S BLACK CAT MILD**
2. **RUDGATE RUBY MILD**

BROWN ALE

One of the oldest of the British brewing styles, and a relative of such similarly-hued beers as the Flemish oud bruin and the German dunkel lager, brown ale is unsurprisingly defined by a rich maltiness derived from amber and brown grains, giving it flavours ranging from toasted caramel to nuttiness to light chocolate.

COMMON STYLE

- **BROWN ALE:** In modern terms, a not overly hoppy beer sporting soothing malt flavours, often including nuttiness, hence its frequent designation as 'nut brown ale' and moderate strength.
- **SCOTTISH-STYLE ALE:** Typically malty but not sweet, with a low alcohol content and an off-dry to quite dry finish. In many cases this could be considered more a cousin of pale ale than brown ale.
- **HOPPY BROWN ALE ('AMERICAN-STYLE BROWN ALE'):** Although there is evidence that early British brown ales were well-hopped, in modern terms bitterness in brown ale is considered an American trait. Often these combine caramelly malty with citrussy hop.
- **AMBER ALE:** Once a mainstay of the North American craft beer market, is now seen much less often. Typically caramelly and lightly sweet to off-dry, with less malt character than a brown ale.
- **ALTBIER:** The dark-hued, northern German yin to kölsch's yang, this native Düsseldorf beer is likewise warm fermented and then cold conditioned for an off-dry to dry character and earthy palate.

FRINGE STYLE

Oatmeal Brown Ale: a mostly American trend – with the potential to grown into a legitimate style – that sees oats added to the mash for a more silken mouthfeel); Imperial altbier (high-strength altbier, often boasting little in common with the original style).

KEY BEERS

1. Brown ale: **BLACK OAK NUT BROWN ALE, SAMUEL SMITH NUT BROWN ALE**
2. Scottish-style ale: **BELHAVEN 80/-, SUN KING WEE MAC SCOTTISH STYLE ALE**
3. Hoppy brown ale ('American-style brown ale'): **BROOKLYN BROWN ALE, SMUTTYNOSE OLD BROWN DOG ALE**
4. Amber Ale: **BATH ALES GEM, DEVIL'S CANYON DEADICATED AMBER, FISH TALE ORGANIC AMBER ALE**
5. Altbier: **UERIGE, SCHUMACHER**

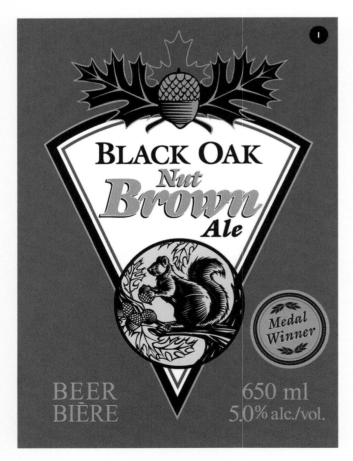

DARK LAGER

The oldest class of lagers, save perhaps for rauchbier, and once ubiquitous in southern Germany and beyond. Nowadays it exists mainly on the stylistic fringes, since dark lagers were supplanted by their pale brethren in the latter 1800s and have not yet recovered in popularity.

COMMON STYLE

- **DUNKEL LAGER:** Ranging from moderately sweet to quite dry, these brown lagers – dunkel is German for 'dark' – can have earthy or caramelly malt notes, but minimal to no fruitiness.
- **SCHWARZBIER:** A black or near-black lager style with flavours similar to those of a stout, but without that style's roundness or fullness of body. Off-dry to dry roasty taste, occasionally accented by liquorice notes.
- **DARK/AMBER LAGER:** Catch-all designation for a host of lagers, from mass-market brands given a darker hue through the use of toasted malts or the addition of caramel, to sweet and generally simple and straight-forward brews and traditional Czech and Czech-inspired lagers with impressive complexity.

KEY BEERS

1. Dunkel lager: **KALTENBERG KÖNIG LUDWIG DUNKEL, AYINGER ALTBAIRISCH DUNKEL**
2. Schwarzbier: **KOSTRITZER, BREZNAK SCHWARZBIER**
3. Dark/Amber lager: **BERNARD CERNÝ LEŽÁK, CAPITAL BREWERY WISCONSIN AMBER**

VERY DARK AND ROASTY ALES

ROASTED BARLEY OR BLACK MALT IS KEY TO THE AROMA AND FLAVOUR OF THIS QUITE SINGULAR CLASS OF ALES, THE CHARACTERS OF WHICH MOST OFTEN SPEAK TO SOME OR ALL OF A QUARTET OF FLAVOURS COMPRISED OF COFFEE, ROAST, BLACK LIQUORICE AND SMOKINESS, SOMETIMES WITH CHOCOLATE NOTES THROWN IN AS WELL.

STOUT/PORTER

Originally porter, which evolved as a darker form of brown ale and stout porter, or strong porter. Today these two basic styles are almost interchangeable. Their variants, however, are legion.

COMMON STYLES

- **LONDON PORTER:** The oldest interpretation of the porter/stout family, with a mild but fruity sweetness and roasted malt flavours, finishing dry or off-dry.
- **PORTER:** A beer very similar to dry stout, with flavours of roasted malt, coffee, liquorice and sometimes a light smokiness.
- **BALTIC PORTER:** Developed when the lager-producing breweries of the Baltics wanted to emulate the Imperial stout style. Lager-fermented and generally thinner and sweeter than the Imperial stout, with a refreshing quality that belies its typically high strength.
- **DRY STOUT/IRISH STYLE STOUT:** Dry and roasty beer with often a lower alcoholic strength of about 4–4.5% ABV and flavours of roasted coffee bean and dark chocolate.
- **OATMEAL STOUT:** Dry stout base made sweeter and silkier through the addition of oats to the mash.
- **IMPERIAL STOUT:** Strong style of stout made popular through exports to Russia and the Baltic regions. Modern versions tend to be sweet and very rich, with roasted malt and cooked fruit flavours and, ideally, a high degree of flavour complexity.

FRINGE STYLE

White Stout: golden ales using flavourings such as coffee and chocolate in an attempt to mimic stout flavours.

KEY BEERS

1. London porter: **MEANTIME LONDON PORTER, FULLER'S LONDON PORTER**
2. Porter: **DESCHUTES BLACK BUTTE PORTER, OH! LA! HO! BEER PORTER**
3. Baltic porter: **TROIS MOUSQUETAIRES PORTER BALTIQUE, OKOCIM PORTER**
4. Dry Stout/Irish-style stout: **O'HARA'S STOUT, TITANIC STOUT**
5. Oatmeal stout: **ANDERSON VALLEY BARNEY FLATS OATMEAL STOUT, MCAUSLAN ST. AMBROISE OATMEAL STOUT**
6. Imperial stout: **KERNEL IMPERIAL BROWN STOUT LONDON 1856, DEL DUCATO VERDI IMPERIAL STOUT**

SMOKED MALT BEERS

POSSIBLY THE SINGLE MOST POLARIZING CATEGORY OF BEER, THESE ALES AND LAGERS RANGE FROM LIGHTLY SMOKY TO AN EFFECT SOMETIMES DESCRIBED AS 'SMOKED HAM IN A GLASS'. FOR THE PATIENT DRINKER, HOWEVER, THE THIRD OR FOURTH ENCOUNTER IS OFTEN WHEN SCEPTICISM TURNS TO GREAT AFFECTION.

SMOKED MALT BEER

When malt was commonly kilned over wood fires, beers tended towards smoky, sometimes meaty flavours. These holdover brews employ carefully smoked malts for the same effect, which ranges from faint campfire notes to intense and enduring smokiness.

COMMON STYLES

- **RAUCHBIER:** Connected to the German city of Bamberg, rauchbiers are amber to dark lagers and märzens, occasionally also weissbiers, with varying degrees of smokiness.

- **SMOKED PORTER/STOUT:** The New World adaptation of the Bamberg rauchbier resulted in a wave of stouts and porters made with smoked malts. Varying degrees of smokiness accentuate the roasty character of the malts already used for such styles.

- **PEATED MALT BEER:** Originating in France, these are beers that use malts dried over peat smoke – typically used for Scottish whisky production – to add smoky, earthy, phenolic flavours to lagers or ales. Sometimes incorrectly identified with Scotch ales, which do not traditionally employ such malts.

- **GRODZISKIE/GRÄTZER:** A historic eastern European style associated most directly with Poland, once forgotten but now making a bit of a comeback. Smoked wheat and a specific sort of yeast give it a light, spritzy and refreshing character.

KEY BEERS

1. Rauchbier: **AECHT SCHLENKERLA RAUCHBIER MÄRZEN, SPEZIAL RAUCHBIER LAGER**
2. Smoked Porter/Stout: **ALASKAN BREWING CO. SMOKED PORTER, SØGAARDS STOUT NOIRE**
3. Peated Malt Beer: **UNIBROUE RAFTMAN, ADELSCOTT**
4. Grodziskie/Grätzer: **PINTA GRODZISKIE**

STRONG AND RICHLY MALTY BEERS

SOOTHING

BREWED FROM AMPLE AMOUNTS OF MALT AND FERMENTED TO HIGH STRENGTH, THESE SWEET AND SEDUCTIVE ALES AND LAGERS ARE THE BEER WORLD'S EQUIVALENT OF A WARMING GLASS OF BRANDY OR PORT, ALTHOUGH MANY ARE AT HOME AT THE DINNER TABLE IN A WAY THOSE DRINKS COULD NEVER BE.

BOCKS/DOPPELBOCK

Strong and malty lagers said to have originated in Einbeck, Germany, and sold in Munich where the name 'Einbeckerbier' is said to have become bockbier over time.

COMMON STYLES

- **BOCK:** At roughly 6% ABV or greater, strong lagers that emphasize plenty of malty sweetness. Typically amber or brown in colour, pale golden bocks also exist and are sometimes known as maibocks.
- **DOPPELBOCK:** Of monastic origin, where their exaggerated maltiness was equated with greater nutritional value, these are stronger and maltier versions of bock, usually of 7% ABV or greater.
- **EISBOCK:** A style of concentrated doppelbock in which the finished brew is cooled until the frozen water might be extracted.

KEY BEERS

1. Bock: **EINBECKER UR-BOCK HELL, NEW GLARUS UFF-DA BOCK**
2. Doppelbock: **AYINGER CELEBRATOR, WELTENBURGER KLOSTER ASAM BOCK**
3. Eisbock: **KULMBACHER EISBOCK**

ABBEY-STYLE STRONG DARK ALE

A broad category of ales originating in the abbeys of northern Europe, where they were thought of as more nutritious beers suitable for serving to honoured guests on feast days, and for drinking during fasting periods.

COMMON STYLES

- **DUBBEL:** Strongly malt-driven ales, amber to deep brown in colour and often sporting flavours of caramel or chocolate, dark fruits and brown spice. Occasionally they are actually brewed with spice.
- **STRONG DARK ALE:** Very strong, often winey or port-like interpretations of the dubbel style.

FRINGE STYLE

Quadruppel: frequently abbreviated as simply 'quad', this term originated at the Koningshoeven Trappist abbey of the Netherlands in the 1990s but is often applied to beers which predate that brewery's La Trappe Quadruppel brand by many decades. In truth, less a fringe style and more a simple misnomer.

KEY BEERS

4. Dubbel: **WESTMALLE DUBBEL, OMMEGANG ABBEY ALE**
5. Strong dark ale: **LA TRAPPE QUADRUPEL, ROCHEFORT 10**

SCOTCH ALE

In the 18th century Scottish brewers were best known for strong and malty ales, sometimes known as Edinburgh ales, however over time those faded in popularity as Scottish beers grew generally weaker. The style was preserved by the Belgians, however, and eventually found its way back to Scotland to become once again the nation's signature style.

COMMON STYLES

- **SCOTCH ALE:** Strong at 7% ABV or better, these ales are characterized by a concentrated maltiness, with flavours resembling cooked toffee or molasses, and very little in the way of bitterness.

FRINGE STYLE

Peated Scotch ale: Scotch ale brewed under the mistaken assumption that Scots make beer from the same peat-smoked malts they use for whisky.

KEY BEERS

1. Scotch ale: **TRAQUAIR HOUSE ALE, RENAISSANCE STONECUTTER SCOTCH ALE**

TRADITIONAL BARLEY WINE/OLD ALE

The British tradition of strong ales dates back centuries, to a time when the strongest beer brewed at a farmhouse brewery would be considered its 'barley wine', or a beer of typical wine strength. The style was first commercialized by Bass, nearly died off in the 20th century and has staged a massive, US-led comeback in the last few decades.

COMMON STYLES

- **BRITISH-STYLE BARLEY WINE:** Strong and malty sweet, usually 7%-8% ABV or greater, with often dominant fruitiness and great malt-driven complexity.
- **OLD ALE:** Similar to British-style barley wine, but specifically crafted for ageing in the cellar and thus often cloyingly sweet when young.
- **AMERICAN-STYLE BARLEY WINE:** A much hoppier interpretation of the barley wine style, often with double digit alcoholic strength and forceful bitterness. Some examples require years of ageing before a balance between hops and malt is found.
- **WHEAT WINE:** Thinner and generally less hoppy than American-style barley wines, but usually just as strong and with a notable citrussy quality from the wheat used.

KEY BEERS

2. British-style barley wine: **ORKNEY SKULL SPLITTER, ALLEY KAT OLDE DEUTERONOMY BARLEY WINE**
3. Old Ale: **J W LEE'S HARVEST ALE, AMSTERDAM BREWING VICAR'S VICE**
4. American-style barley wine: **ANCHOR OLD FOGHORN, AVERY HOG HEAVEN BARLEY WINE**
5. Wheat Wine: **BOULEVARD HARVEST DANCE**

2

3

4

5

TART, SPONTANEOUS OR MIXED FERMENTATION BEERS

SURPRISINGLY, THE BEVERAGE CLOSEST IN CHARACTER TO MANY OF THESE BREWS IS NOT BEER, BUT DRY CHAMPAGNE. USUALLY SPRITZY AND OFTEN QUITE ASTONISHING IN THEIR TARTNESS, THEY ARE IDEALLY SUITED TO THE ROLE OF APERITIF, ALTHOUGH THEY OFTEN SHOW A HIGH DEGREE OF VERSATILITY AT THE TABLE AS WELL.

LAMBIC

Beers made from a mash comprised of roughly one third unmalted wheat, seasoned with aged hops that contribute no bitterness, only preservative qualities, then spontaneously fermented and aged in wooden barrels.

COMMON STYLES
- **STRAIGHT LAMBIC (RARE IN BOTTLE):** Mildly tart and lightly carbonated, months-old lambic beer, known for its highly refreshing nature and wheaty character.
- **GUEUZE LAMBIC:** Lambics of between one and three years of age, blended and bottle-fermented to a satisfyingly tart, champagne-like dryness, often with tangy, lemony qualities.

FRINGE STYLE

Sweetened Gueuze: large production gueuze lambic beers that have been heavily sweetened with saccharine or fruit juice to take the edge off the style's typical tartness.

KEY BEERS
1. Straight lambic (rare in bottle): **CANTILLON GRAND CRU BRUOCSELLA 1900**
2. Gueuze lambic: **LINDEMAN CUVÉE RENÉ, DE CAM GUEUZE**

NEW WORLD MIXED FERMENTATION

A wide array of beers, ranging from wheat beers spontaneously-fermented in the Swiss Alps or on the Maine coast to so-called 'wild' IPAs to all manner of beer styles aged in wild yeast- and/or bacteria-inoculated barrels.

COMMON STYLES

This is a family for which it is rather pointless to even attempt a list of styles, since almost any type of beer, from light wheats to intense stouts, may be subjected to a mixed fermentation. Increasingly, these beers are classed in an awkward and outrageously diverse grouping known as 'sour beers'.

KEY BEERS

3. **NEW BELGIUM LA FOLIE** or anything from Oregon's **CASCADE BREWING BARREL HOUSE**

FLEMISH STYLE RED AND BROWN ALES

Inspired by the barrel-ageing of English porters, Belgian brewers in the north have long been ageing red and brown ales in wooden vats of varying sizes. The resident bacteria within contribute tartness and occasionally very strong berry fruit flavours to the beers.

COMMON STYLES

- **FLEMISH RED ALE:** Traditionally aged in large wooden tuns, but not necessarily so these days, these are oaky beers with tart and profoundly fruity flavours and a dry, acidic finish.
- **FLEMISH BROWN ALE:** Close cousin to the Flemish red, these are generally less fruity and more sweet and tart in character, with oaky and caramel flavours and a sweeter finish.

KEY BEERS

1. Flemish Red Ale: **RODENBACH GRAND CRU, DUCHESSE DU BOURGOGNE**
2. Flemish Brown Ale: **LIEFMANS GOUDENBAND, OERBIER RESERVA**

REFRESHING AND LIGHT-BODIED WHEAT BEERS

WHERE IT IS STILL CONSIDERED SOCIALLY ACCEPTABLE TO DRINK A BEER BEFORE NOON, THESE GENTLE YET QUITE FLAVOURFUL WHEATS ARE SOMETIMES THOUGHT OF AS 'BREAKFAST BEERS', OR AT LEAST 'BRUNCH BREWS'. FOR THOSE UNFAMILIAR WITH BEER BEYOND THE PALE LAGER, THEY CAN ALSO BE A MOST AGREEABLE INTRODUCTION.

BERLINER WEISSE

Now almost extinct in Germany, but growing in popularity elsewhere, this beer is fermented with yeast in conjunction with lactobacillus, yielding a clean and crisp acidity and typically a very low alcohol content.

COMMON STYLE

- **BERLINER WEISSE:** Very low alcohol content of +/- 3% ABV and a tart, tangy, pleasantly 'spoiled cream' flavour profile, often moderated by the addition of sweet fruit syrups.

KEY BEERS

1. Berliner weiss: **NEW GLARUS BERLINER WEISSE, PROFESSOR FRITZ BRIEM 1809 BERLINER STYLE WEISSE**

BELGIAN-STYLE WHEAT BEER

Beer comprised of one third or more unmalted wheat and flavoured with orange peel and coriander, plus occasionally other spices.

COMMON STYLE

- **WITBIER/BIERE BLANCHE/WHITE BEER:** Very light in colour and on the palate, with varying degrees of orange and coriander flavours and a citrus effervescence.

KEY BEERS

1. Witbier/Bière blanche/White beer: **BLANCHE DE NAMUR, ALLAGASH WHITE**

GERMAN-STYLE WHEAT BEER

A range of ales brewed from mashes comprised of upwards of 50% malted wheat and fermented by one of a family of yeasts that typically imparts flavours and aromas of banana and clove.

COMMON STYLES

- **HEFEWEIZEN/WEISSBIER/HEFEWEISSBIER:** Usually light-hued beers with an effervescent nature, lightly sweet character and varying degrees of spicy (clove, black pepper) and fruity (banana) notes.
- **DUNKELWEIZEN/DUNKEL WEISSBIER:** Like a weissbier, but with darker malts added to the mix for a more caramelly or earthy, and sometimes spicier, flavour profile.
- **KRISTAL WEISSBIER:** A filtered version of the hefeweissbier – 'hefe' means yeast and indicates bottle-fermentation – with a slightly to significantly less spicy and fruity and often more lemony flavour profile.
- **GOSE:** Previously obscure beer style identified with the town of Leipzig, it is characterized by its most unconventional ingredient, salt, which adds varying degrees of saltiness to a light-bodied and lemony wheat beer.

FRINGE STYLE

Hefeweizen: The term is sometimes used in the United States to indicate an unfiltered American wheat ale without the banana and clove typical of the German yeast profile.

KEY BEERS

1. Hefeweizen/Weissbier/Hefeweissbier: **SCHNEIDER WEISSE TAP 7 UNSER ORIGINAL, WEIHENSTEPHANER HEFEWEISSBIER**
2. Dunkelweizen/Dunkel weissbier: **WEIHENSTEPHANER HEFEWEISSBIER DUNKEL, FRANZISKANER HEFE-WEISSE DUNKEL**
3. Gose: **WESTBROOK GOSE, BAYERISCHER BAHNHOF LEIPZIGER GOSE**
4. Kristal weissbier: **MAISEL'S WEISSE KRISTALL, BISCHOFSHOF KRISTALL WEIZEN**

NORTH AMERICAN-STYLE WHEAT BEER

In the early days of North American craft brewing, wheat was added to pale malt mashes to make a wheat ale that might appeal to a lager drinker.

COMMON STYLE

- **WHEAT ALE**: golden in colour and usually without much complexity, the distinguishing feature in some is a light lemony character derived from the wheat.

KEY BEER

1. Wheat ale: **R&B SUN GOD WHEAT ALE**

SPICY AND SPICED BEERS

SPICY

AS ENIGMATIC A COLLECTION OF BEERS AS EXISTS, THE SELF-DESCRIBING SPICINESS OF THESE BREWS CAN RANGE FROM A GENTLE CLOVE OR BLACK PEPPER NOTE STEMMING FROM FERMENTATION TO WHAT SOMETIMES SEEMS LIKE AN ENTIRE KITCHEN CABINET-FULL OF SPICES AND HERBS ADDED DIRECTLY TO THE BEER.

GERMAN STYLE WEIZENBOCK

A fusion of two great German beer styles, doppelbock and weissbier, producing one powerhouse of a spicy, fruity style.

COMMON STYLE

- **WEIZENBOCK:** The spiciness and banana quality of a dunkelweizen amped up in a higher alcohol, often quite a bit darker ale. Usually more spicy than fruity, although spices are never added.

KEY BEER

1. Weizenbock: **AVENTINUS, MAHRS BRAU DER WEISSE BOCK**

SPICED ALE

A mixed bag of beers flavoured with all manner of herbs and spices, sometimes in combination with fruit or honey.

COMMON STYLES

- **BELGIAN-STYLE SPICED ALE:** Belgian brewers, and those emulating them, will use such a grab-bag of spices in such different and diverse ways, from subtle background hints to in-your-face spice cake, that it is pointless to even try to list off relevant styles. Suffice to say that the most common are malt- rather than hop-driven ales.
- **NEW WORLD SPICED BEER:** Like the Belgian style, this class encompasses a diverse mix of styles. The difference is that the beers can be ales, lagers or mixed fermentation beers and the spices used can include such atypical ingredients as chillies, tobacco leaf and yerba mate.
- **SAHTI:** Traditional Finnish farmhouse ale brewed with barley malts and other assorted grains, often rye. Fermented by baker's yeast and filtered through a bed

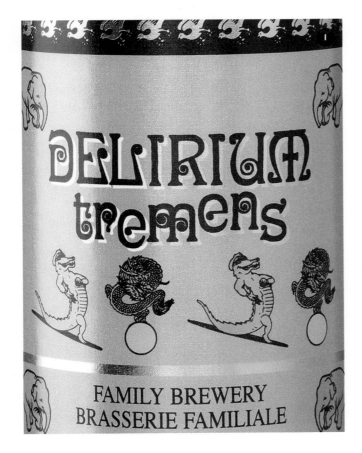

of juniper branches, and often unhopped, sahti develops a higher than average strength and a spicy-sweet, fruity, tannic character that is best when as fresh as possible.

KEY BEERS

1. Belgian-style Spiced Ale: **DELIRIUM TREMENS, FANTÔME SPECIAL NOEL**
2. New World Spiced Beer: **HOP BACK TAIPHOON LEMON GRASS BEER, MATE VEZA YERBA MATE IPA**

FRUIT-DEFINED BEERS

FRUITY

OFTEN DERIDED AS BEING LESS THAN 'REAL BEER', IN COMMON WITH THEIR SPICED KIN, THESE BEERS SPEAK TO A DAY BEFORE HOPS WERE COMMON IN BREWING, WHEN ALL MANNER OF FRUITS WERE EMPLOYED INSTEAD. THEIR FLAVOURS MAY RANGE FROM THE DRY ESSENCE OF A BERRY TO A SWEET, FULL-FRONTAL FRUITY ASSAULT.

FRUIT LAMBIC

While spontaneously-fermented lambics are still ageing, brewers will drop large quantities of whole fruit into the barrel, thus stimulating a new fermentation and flavouring the beer with the driest qualities of the fruit.

COMMON STYLES

- **KRIEK:** Following a second fermentation with whole cherries, these beers emerge with a reddish tinge and a dryly fruity character, often accented by almond notes from the cherry pits.
- **FRAMBOISE:** The raspberry version of a fruit lambic, with an extra fruity tartness and light pink fruity hue.

FRINGE STYLE

Sweet fruit lambic: lambic beers sweetened and made fruity by the addition of concentrates, juices, extracts and/or sweeteners.

KEY BEERS

1. Kriek: **3 FONTEINEN OUDE KRIEK, BOON MARIAGE PARFAIT OUDE KRIEK**
2. Framboise: **CANTILLON ROSÉ DE GAMBRINUS, FRAMBOISE BOON**

FRUIT WHEAT BEERS

Early North American craft brewers discovered that they could add another beer to their portfolios by taking their wheat ale and making it into a fruit beer, either by fermenting it with fruit or fruit juice or, simpler still, adding fruit juice or extract to the beer post fermentation.

COMMON STYLES

- **RASPBERRY WHEAT:** While wheat beers have been flavoured with all manner of fruits, raspberries proved so popular for a time that 'Raspberry Beer' was once a category at the Great American Beer Festival.

KEY BEER

3. Raspberry Wheat: **SEA DOG RASPBERRY WHEAT ALE**

FRUITED ALE

Once the infatuation with fruit wheat beers had run its course, brewers in the United States and, eventually, well beyond, began to turn their attention to other beer styles that could be similarly flavoured, giving rise to a wide array of fruit beers of all styles and featuring all sorts of fruits.

COMMON STYLES

- Far too many to mention, with no fruit or fruited style really dominant. Cherry and other fruit stouts are fairly common, but so are mixed fermentation beers featuring various fruits and, particularly in Italy, beers mashed, fermented or aged with grape must left over from winemaking.

KEY BEER

4. **NEW GLARUS WISCONSIN BELGIAN RED**

WILDCARDS

SINCE MODERN BREWING RECOGNIZES NO BOUNDARIES, THERE SEEMS TO BE NO END TO THE NEW STYLES, SUB-STYLES AND RESURRECTED BEERS THAT ARE JOINING THE WORLD OF BEER ON ALMOST A WEEKLY BASIS. THESE BEERS ARE BOUNDLESS, LIMITED ONLY BY THE IMAGINATION OF THE BREWER AND APPETITE OF THE PUBLIC.

What is it that turns a beer into a legitimate style? Innovation? Influence? Ubiquity? Or perhaps some combination of the three?

While it is difficult to determine what exactly turns a popular mix of ingredients or set of techniques into a style of beer, it is safe to say that the standard should be a high one. For otherwise we might find ourselves faced with a world in which every brewer's beer is a 'style' of its own, thus rendering the entire concept of styles effectively useless.

That said, however, there is a handful of trends in brewing that are either sufficiently established or boast sufficient potential to produce a nation's signature style of beer that they should be considered possible styles for the long run. In some cases they are easily defined by a single ingredient, while in others they are more ethereal, but across the board they certainly merit contemplation.

- **BARREL-FLAVOURED BEERS:** Beer has long been stored and aged in wooden barrels, but the practice fell well out of favour with the arrival of stainless steel tanks and kegs. Over the last few decades, however, conditioning beer in barrels that have previously held anything from bourbon to Scotch whisky, Chianti to grappa, and brandy to chardonnay has exploded in popularity. These beers cover all manner of styles and strengths, and in at least one instance – Italy, where wine barrels are growing in usage – may eventually come to serve as a calling card for a nation's craft brewers.

- **PUMPKIN BEER:** Love them or hate them, and there are plenty of people who feel quite strongly either way, pumpkin flavoured beers are likely here to stay. Born of the United States, these beers, frequently flavoured with the gourd plus spices, but often just spiced with the mix of clove, allspice and cinnamon generally used in pumpkin pie, have now gone international and cover base styles that range from pumpkin hefeweizens to pumpkin stouts.

- **COFFEE BEER:** Now in their third decade as a craft brewing ingredient, coffee beans are used in styles from stout to pale ale to dunkel lager, with intensities ranging from mild and faintly coffee-ish to intense and espresso-like.
- **AMAZONIAN BEER:** The Amazon yields a wealth of woods and fruits virtually unknown to people outside of South America, but well understood by the brewers of Brazil. Thus it is with fruits like the jabuticaba and woods such as amburana, popular with cachaça producers, that Brazilian craft brewing may yet make its international mark.
- **NEW ZEALAND/AOTEAROA PILSNER AND PALE ALE:** These beers, styled respectively after the Czech-style pilsner and American-style pale ale, use New Zealand varieties of hops to produce typically tropical fruit aromas and flavours.
- **RYE PALE ALE/RYE P.A:** These increasingly popular variants on American-style pale ale and IPA employ healthy amounts of rye in their mashes to produce distinctly spicy flavour profiles.

KEY BEERS

1. Barrel-flavoured beers: **THE LOST ABBEY CUVÉE DE TOMME, DE MOLEN BOMMEN & GRANATEN**
2. Pumpkin beer: **DOGFISH HEAD PUNKIN, ELYSIAN THE GREAT PUMPKIN**
3. Coffee beer: **MIKKELLER BEER GEEK BRUNCH WEASEL, ALESMITH SPEEDWAY STOUT**
4. Amazonian beer: **CERVEJARIA WAY AMBURANA LAGER, AMAZON BEER FOREST**
5. Rye pale ale/Rye P.A.: **SIERRA NEVADA RUTHLESS RYE, CAMERON'S RYE.P.A.**
6. New Zealand/Aotearoa pilsner and Pale ale: **TUATARA AOTEAROA PALE ALE, EMERSON'S PILSNER**

BEER AND FOOD BEFORE THE 21ST CENTURY

WHERE IT ALL BEGAN

THE PAIRING OF BEER AND FOOD IS NOT NEARLY SO NEW A CONCEPT AS IS SOMETIMES THOUGHT. BEER HAS BEEN IN EXISTENCE FOR AT LEAST 10,000 YEARS AFTER ALL, AND HUMAN BEINGS HAVE, BY DEFINITION, BEEN EATING FOR MUCH LONGER THAN THAT. SO IT'S ONLY LOGICAL THAT THE TWO WOULD HAVE MET, MATCHED AND BECOME INTERTWINED ALONG THE WAY.

It's just that while all of this was going on, our ancestors weren't really aware of what they were doing.

As humans, we are the only animals on the planet capable of gastronomy, alone in our ability to take a variety of edible things – vegetables, spices, meat and liquids – and mix them together to create what we call a dish. We've done this for millennia and we continue to do it today, whether it's something as simple as steamed broccoli with salt and butter, or as complicated as modern-day molecular cuisine.

When our ancestors were merely eating in order to survive, the ingredients they put together and the methods in which they did so were pretty basic. Mix fava beans together with oil, cumin and garlic, for instance, and you have *Ful Medames*, an Egyptian dish that some food experts hypothesise about dating back to the time of the Pharaohs. Google 'biblical recipes' and you'll probably find Tiger Nut Sweets, a mix of dates, nuts, cinnamon and honey. And you can bet that the our long-ago ancestors were grilling meats over an open fire pretty much as is, without the benefit of careful seasoning or a celebrity-endorsed barbecue sauce.

AS TIME PROGRESSED, NATIONAL CUISINES BEGAN TO BE FORMED, AND ALONGSIDE THEM, NATIONAL BEER STYLES. NOT SURPRISINGLY, THE TWO WERE OFTEN CONSUMED TOGETHER, AND THUS PAIRINGS WERE ALSO BORN.

Perhaps not entirely conscious pairings, but certainly pairings nonetheless.

Whether cuisines evolved to reflect the beers being brewed at the time or the beers adjusted to the popular dishes we will likely never know – although the latter seems more likely, given the way in which beer styles have changed through the years – but certainly a number of national food and beer pairing conventions have been formed over the course of the past centuries. Most of them will come as no surprise, indeed you are most likely to have experienced several examples of each yourself, but it's what we can learn from them that is important.

LEFT The Princess Louise in Holborn, London is a perfectly preserved example of a typical 'gin palace' of the Victorian era.

OPPOSITE Fishermen share a libation in mid-19th century Britain.

The very first meal I enjoyed during my first-ever trip to London was fish and chips, the quintessential pub staple. Except that I didn't eat it in an actual pub. I bought it, paper wrapped, from a stand located not far off Leicester Square. And I didn't drink cask-conditioned best bitter alongside it, as is traditional, but Champagne, because I was both celebrating and had arrived after the pubs closed.

BEER AND FOOD DESTINATION

THE GRAIN BARGE IN BRISTOL HAS PUB GRUB WHICH IS A CUT ABOVE THE USUAL, SERVED IN AN INFORMAL ATMOSPHERE ALONGSIDE A RANGE OF SOLID BUT INTERESTING BEERS FROM A GREAT LOCAL BREWERY, THE BRISTOL BEER FACTORY.

JESSICA BOAK AND RAY BAILEY ('BOAK & BAILEY'), PROLIFIC BEER BLOGGERS AND AUTHORS OF *BREW BRITANNIA*

There's a story behind the Champagne, but more of that later (see page 73). For now, let's return to fish and chips.

While the exact location where battered and deep-fried fish was first combined with similarly fried strips of potato remains a matter of some conjecture and debate, it is generally agreed that the momentous event occurred sometime in the 1860s. This would position the genesis of the dish and its rapid growth in popularity at around the same time as the concurrent decline of porter and the rise of pale ale and IPA in England.

It would be folly to suggest that the popularization of pale ales in England, and especially around London, had anything to do with what the *Oxford Companion to Food* refers to as the steady growth in the number of fish and chip shops up until the start of World War Two, but the fact remains that pale ale and best bitter did grow to dominate English beer sales during that same period. And like many foods and beverages that evolved alongside one another, they do pair together marvellously well.

In a similar vein, although more than a century earlier, back when oysters both raw and cooked were popular snacks in the drinking houses of London, porter was at the height of its great popularity. Did one foretell the other? Most assuredly not, but if you've ever sat down to a plate of oysters on the half shell and a pint of good porter or stout, you will understand why the former had more than just low cost and bountiful abundance to commend it.

The same goes for what we today consider to be classic English pub fare. Steak and kidney pie may have fallen a bit out of favour these days, but it's still a delightful partner to pints of best bitter, ESB or brown ale, depending on the richness and intensity of the gravy. Cumberland sausage and mashed potatoes or chips is a superior dish when served with a pint of best bitter or stronger ESB, as is a properly assembled ploughman's lunch, always with a healthy chunk of good Cheddar cheese. Even the full English breakfast, with sausage, bacon, eggs, beans and so much more, is made more enticing by the addition of a glass of low-strength ordinary bitter and is perhaps also a tad more easy to digest.

Such dishes did not suddenly begin appearing on pub menus everywhere overnight. They, like the beers which accompany them, evolved over time into staples of the cuisine, and their staying power is most likely attributable to, among other strengths, a strong compatibility with the same beers.

Which brings us to the first lesson of pre-21st century beer and food pairing. If the beer and the cuisine 'grew up' together, then they most likely will pair well together. Always with the caveat that this tenet works best in nations with long and varied histories of brewing and beer culture, such as England. Or Germany.

ABOVE The Barton Arms in Aston, Birmingham, is one of the finest examples of Victorian pub architecture in the UK.

OPPOSITE The origin of fish and chips is said to date back to the 1860s. Nowadays it is an iconic dish in the British pub, together with steak and ale pie and the ploughman's lunch.

It requires little time spent in the south of Germany to reach the conclusion that Bavarians are very fond of pork. From the traditional pork knuckle known as *Schweinshaxe*, or sometimes just *Hax'n*, to sausages, roast pork and schnitzels, pig abounds on beer hall menus across Bavaria and deep into the north of the country too.

It might take even less time, however, to realize that the Bavarian beer playing field is essentially dominated by a trio of blonde beer styles: helles, weissbier and pils, with supporting roles played by significantly lower-volume players such as dunkel lager, bock and doppelbock, dunkel weissbier and weizenbock, Oktoberfest märzen and, of course, the smoked rauchbiers of Franconia, plus other assorted seasonal and regional specialities.

Take a minute to review those beer styles above and you will find something pretty close to a common thread in that, save for the wheat beers, all are lagers.

Lager brewing was not always the default position for Teutonic brewmasters, just as the nearly uniform pale expression of helles and pils and weissbier was not always the expected colour of German beers. But as lager fermentation quickly came to dominate following its accidental discovery in the Alpine caves where Bavarians used to store their beers for summer, so too did the pale hue of the original pilsner, brewed in 1842 in the Czech town of Pilsen. The popularity of pilsner soared rapidly among brewers in Bohemia and Bavaria first, followed by northern Germany and the surrounding nations, and then finally throughout the world.

Coincidentally, the 19th century also witnessed a change in the way pork was eaten. Rather than being served at celebrations in the form of a whole suckling pig, pork was now consumed more regularly along with beef and veal, later becoming the main meat at a Bavarian table.

Which brings us back to our plate of *Hax'n* and the one litre *Maß* of golden helles served alongside it. Eyeing warily its craggy, hard-shelled exterior and the sharp, broad-bladed knife that protrudes intimidatingly from its core, it's easy to convince yourself that there is no way in the brewhouse or beyond that this pale, delicate-looking lager could possibly stand up to the flavours on the plate. But even still, you cut – or rather, carve – until you breach the armour-like crackling and reach the moist meat inside, slice off a mouthful, follow it with a gulp of beer... heaven!

At the next meal, it might be pork schnitzel and pils. And at the one after that, roast pork loin with weissbier, admittedly an ale rather than a lager, but with a countenance closer to that of a helles or pils than, say, a pale ale or porter. Then pork sausage and helles again, or dunkel if the wurst is served with gravy. And through it all, the partnerships blend together quite marvellously.

Of course, this reflects what was learned from pub cuisine in that both pork and pale lager and wheat beer grew in popularity together, but there is more to the Bavarian lesson than just that.

SIMPLY, THE RULE HERE IS THAT WHEN PORK APPEARS ON THE TABLE, YOU JUST CAN'T GO TOO FAR WRONG IF YOU CHOOSE A GERMAN STYLE OF BEER AS ITS ACCOMPANIMENT, BE IT PALE LAGER, DARK WHEAT BEER OR POTENT DOPPELBOCK.

Or in other words, as I have long noted with a grin during tastings and beer dinners, the Bavarian brewer whose beer does not pair well with pork is a brewer who will not be in business for long.

OPPOSITE The Löwenbräu-Festzelt is one of the seven big tents at the annual Munich Oktoberfest beer festival held each October.

ABOVE LEFT German steins are synonymous with German lagers and come in 500ml (17 ½ fl oz) and more typical 1 litre (35fl oz) measures.

ABOVE RIGHT Platters of cheese and cold or hot pork dishes are the staple of beer hall cusine, complementing German beer perfectly.

No one who has visited Belgium for more than a train or plane change could fail to notice the intense relationship this diminutive nation has with its beer. As wine is to France or Italy, beer is to Belgium, and with very good reason. For while the country neither produces nor consumes the most beer per capita in the world, it is unquestionably responsible for some of the most interesting brews.

Although it has become common of late in some circles to refer to 'Belgian-style' beers – usually referring to an ale fermented with a yeast that is prone to the creation of spicy or funky aromas and flavours – there really is no such thing as a Belgian style of beer. For how could such a thing possibly exist when the country's brews range from tart and Champagne-like gueuze lambics to rich, strong and ponderously malty Trappist ales and pale, international lagers to formidable spiced beers? Simply, it could not.

BEER AND FOOD DESTINATION

'MY BEST PLACE FOR FOOD AND GOOD BEERS IS T'HOMMELHOF AT WATOU, BELGIUM. THE CHEF, STEFAAN COUTTENYE, IS ONE OF THE BEST IN BELGIUM, AND THE RESTAURANT HAS A VERY NICE ATMOSPHERE AND A WONDERFUL BEER MENU.'
MANUELE COLONA, OWNER OF BIR & FUD AND MA CHE SIETE VENUTI A FA', ITALY

And this is, in fact, Belgium's greatest strength when it comes to beer. Diversity is the watchword of Belgian brewing, to the point where legend has it a Belgian brewer, when asked what style their beer might be, will reply 'my style'. There scarcely exists a basic beer flavour profile that is not met in 'Het Biercountry'.

There is, however, one point that the majority of Belgian beers do have in common: most are highly desirable mealtime partners.

While German and Czech beers (see page 70) are mostly studies in contrast, Belgian beers tend to complement the dishes they are served alongside, sometimes in tanginess, other times in richness and certainly on occasion in fruitiness or their chocolate nature. This extends even to the kitchen, where Belgian chefs are known to make very effective use of the panoply of beer flavours at their disposal, employing them as fundamental ingredients in a host of dishes.

This close kinship of beer and food is apparent at almost any traditionally-minded restaurant in Belgium, where you are likely to find such options as the beef stew known as *carbonnades Flamandes*, always simmered for hours in beer; *waterzooi* of chicken or fish, a sort of soup-stew with a broth made of stock, cream and sometimes ale; and rabbit cooked in beer, often a tart gueuze, but sometimes a rich and malty dubbel. Any of these dishes will pair well with beer, and although I frequently counsel against it as a default position, often the best beer pairing for each will be the beer used in the dish's preparation.

Switch the focus to cheese, a severely under-appreciated speciality of the country, and you'll find a beer for every Belgian cheese and a cheese for every Belgian beer. Try a traditional gueuze lambic with an equally tangy, youthful goat's milk cheese, perhaps adding a sliced radish or two and a sprinkle of salt alongside, or an indulgent triple cream cheese with a malty dubbel of strength and refinement. Funky flavours in beer with funky flavours in cheese, pungent and pungent, richness matched with richness; the list continues.

Contrasts to all of the foods listed above do, of course, exist, and a sharp Flemish red ale can make a lovely counterpoint to the sweet nuttiness of an aged gouda, just as a hoppy pilsner or a dry and spicy golden ale can cut the creaminess of a *waterzooi*. But when it comes to Belgian cuisine and, indeed, many such assertively flavourful dishes, these relationships are generally less reliable than their complementary alternatives.

OPPOSITE ABOVE AND BELOW RIGHT Moules marinières accompanied by frites and a Belgian witbier to drink is one of the perfect beer and food pairings – effortless and satisfying.

OPPOSITE BELOW LEFT De Dolle Arabier is a pure malt beer of 8% ABV that is dry hopped during the brewing process.

In the late 1990s, I spent some time in the Czech Republic, dividing my time between Prague and Pilsen. My focus being, quite naturally, on beer, I spent a considerable amount of time drinking and eating in Czech beer halls, from old Prague mainstays like U Medvídku and the iconic U Fleků to the then-pioneering brewpub, Pivovarský Dům, and, of course, the Na Spilce Restaurant at the Pilsner Urquell brewery.

Along the way, I became very much acquainted with the basics of Czech beer-drinking cuisine. I also grew about seven pounds heavier.

Not entirely dissimilar to what is popular with their Bavarian neighbours, Czech beer hall cuisine favourites include dishes that are heavy on meats, from pork to chicken and beef, although with a greater emphasis on stews and sauces. By my calculations however, it was not the generous portions that contributed to the growing tightness of my waistband, and neither was it the richness of the soups and sauces. No, what did me in were the

dumplings. These dumplings, made of bread or potato, respectively *houskový knedlík* and *bramborový knedlík*, are a cornerstone of basic Czech food, with one or the other, or sometimes both, accompanying most dishes. Occasionally you can even score the dumpling 'triple', with a bacon dumpling, špekový *knedlík*, thrown in for good measure.

While you may sometimes come across a recipe for 'light' Czech-style dumplings, in the beer hall such things are purely figments of the imagination. Bread dumplings are dense, potato dumplings more so, and while I still recall with great fondness the flavour of the bacon dumplings I enjoyed, those delicious balls of flavour come with a significant fatty price tag.

OPPOSITE LEFT Roast meat with bread and potato dumplings is a must-try dish in any Czech beer hall or bar.

OPPOSITE RIGHT A favourite tipple the world over, Pilsner Urquell remains one of the best examples of classic Czech lager.

ABOVE The beer garden at the iconic and ever popular brew hall U Fleků in Prague is busy all year round.

After quit some time of eating dumplings with nearly every meal, I was ready for a straight week of salads, maybe quite a bit longer. I've no idea how much worse my state would have been without the ameliorating effects of the copious quantities of Czech lager I used to wash it all down.

While no one can deny the caloric content of beer, the paradox of the Czech beer hall is that the country's pale lagers, of a style we would call pilsners but are there referred to as *světlý*, are ideally suited to providing a refreshing contrast to the weight of the nation's food, from long-simmered goulashes to beef in heavy cream sauce to the ubiquitous dumplings. Their typical hoppiness cuts through the fat, while their dry crispness and quenching nature refreshes both the palate and the spirit, to a degree counteracting the somnolent quality that substantial meals can often have.

Thus illustrating that when it comes to pairing food and beer, sometimes a contrasting relationship can be far superior to the partnership that matches weight to weight and richness to richness.

Although until now we have been addressing nations with many generations of brewing tradition behind them, insight may also be gleaned from a beer culture measured in decades rather than centuries and millennia. Even one in which the height of brewing prowess was at one time – and in some segments, still is – considered to be lager so light, sweetish and anaemic that its flavour is only barely discernible.

While the United States is today rightly considered a hotbed of brewing activity and craft beer innovation, it must be remembered that the nation was at one time a bit of a global joke when it came to beer. During the time when beer drinkers in the US were seemingly obsessed over whether Miller Lite tasted great or was less filling – almost certainly more the latter than the former, it must be noted – the rest of the world was busy disparaging Lite and all its

kin, joking that they were barely beer at all, or, in the immortal words of the Monty Python comedy troupe, 'f**king close to water'.

Even so, those pallid brews did serve a purpose other than bland social lubricant, and the key to their utility was, and remains, the humble bar snack.

American bar food is arguably the most successful and pervasive cuisine in the world, found with relative ease almost anywhere in the western world and often in the east, as well. Whether in London or São Paulo, Munich or Montreal, you won't need to search far to find a bar offering the same sort of fare you'd likely be served in a tavern in Toledo, Ohio or Tempe, Arizona. And the reason for this phenomenon, other than the general global pervasiveness of American culture, is that food's general affinity for and harmony with low flavour, international lagers.

If you were to take an inventory of the quintessential American bar foods, you would find that most, if not all, share one or more of three basic flavour elements: salty, spicy and fatty. Chicken wings are usually both spicy and fatty, if not salty besides; nacho platters offer all three elements; hamburgers are most often fatty and salty, although they can easily be made to be spicy, as well; and the strips of deep-fried chicken known as 'fingers' are certainly salty and fatty and possibly spicy too, depending on what you choose to dip them in.

On the beer side, dealing with the big-selling lagers that make up the international heavyweights of beer sales, that inventory list is much shorter. It is, in truth, limited to pretty much one element, carbonation, which is where we finally return to that Champagne and fish and chips combination I enjoyed during my first ever visit to London (see page 64).

Regardless of whether the big name, big brewery beer in question is almost imperceptibly hoppy or mildly bitter – global lager brands don't really get more than gently hoppy – grainier or maltier, it is the carbonation that will always make the beer a happy partner to typical American bar foods because it acts as a cleanser to help sweep the fat, salt and spice off of the tongue, refreshing the palate and readying it for the next bite.

For the same reason that Champagne, with its infinite supply of tiny bubbles, is considered the ultimate 'goes with anything' wine, suitable for drinking with dishes that might otherwise be difficult, if not impossible, to pair with wine, as fish and chips, highly carbonated lagers are wonderfully adept foils for almost anything salty, spicy or fatty. For the flavour-conscious beer drinker, far better would be a beer with a more assertive nature – a significant hoppiness to help cut the fat or salt or spice, for instance – but for what they are, and for what so much mediocre, stomach-filling bar food is, they and their brisk carbonation certainly do the job well.

OPPOSITE The large tap room at the Firestone Walker brewery in Paso Robles, Northern California, is a favourite craft beer destination. Its adjoining restaurant serves food made with its own beers.

ABOVE LEFT Buffalo wings and beer are a sublime beer and food combination. Highly carbonated lagers sit beautifully alongside such salty, spicy and fatty foods.

ABOVE RIGHT There's nothing more American than a blue-cheese burger topped with bacon, served with fries and accompanied today by a pint of pale ale or IPA.

Beer is a relatively recent arrival to Asia in general and Japan in particular, having only gained a hold in the Land of the Rising Sun sometime around the mid-nineteenth century, yet its grip since then has been a strong one. So much so that, in 1977, pioneering beer writer Michael Jackson was moved to predict that the world's largest brewer may one day be a Japanese one, Kirin.

Although the Americans, the British and the Dutch were all early influencers in the development of the Japanese brewing industry, far and away the greatest inspiration was provided by Germany. It was here that a Japanese government researcher was dispatched in 1869, tasked with finding out more about this newly arrived industry. The German beer hall then became the model upon which dozens of Japanese beer halls were built, including the first ever one in Tokyo's famous Ginza district, installed by the Sapporo brewery in 1899.

BEER AND FOOD DESTINATION

'THE FIRST GREAT BEER AND FOOD PLACE THAT COMES TO MIND IS BAIRD'S TAPROOM – HARAJUKU IN TOKYO. BAIRD'S IS A GREAT CRAFT BREWERY AND THE FOOD SERVED IS TRADITIONAL LIGHT 'IZAKAYA' FARE, MEANING AN ASSORTMENT OF SMALL PLATE DISHES THAT PAIR PERFECTLY WITH THEIR BEERS.'
SCOTT ROBERTSON, HEAD BREWER AT BREWERKZ, SINGAPORE

OPPOSITE ABOVE A typical izakaya is an informal Japanese drinking establishment that serves food to accompany drinks – the Japanese equivalent of a pub – in Osaka, Japan.

OPPOSITE BELOW Sapporo beer signs make a fetching display in the Sapporo Beer Museum in Sapporo, Hokkaido.

ABOVE While 'dry' beers can ably stand alongside more delicate fare, they fall far short when faced with miso and fatty meat. This is more a job for the new generation of Japanese craft beers.

So, Japan has for all of its short life as a brewing power been a land of lagers. Further, it is a nation that has taken lager to perhaps its most delicate interpretation.

Japanese cuisine is, to a great degree, one that prizes nuance. A sampling at an izakaya, for instance, might feature sashimi, edamame and tofu, all foods with fairly gentle and unassertive tastes. If something fried is added to the mix, it will likely be tempura, with a light, fast-fried batter, to highlight the flavour of the ingredients.

All but the gentlest of beverages will overwhelm the flavours of such subtly flavourful foods, which is why saké, with its generally mild character and finely honed complexities, works so well at their sides. This is also why the lager style known as 'dry' was invented in Japan and continues to dominate the country's beer market.

Usually brewed from a mixed mash of barley malt and rice, dry beers are light in a way that American light lagers are not, more finely nuanced and not anywhere near as sweet. In essence they mimic some of the flavours associated with sake, including a soft spiciness and floral and dry grain notes. Dry beer also works better than higher alcohol rice-based sakes over a whole evening at an izakaya.

The Japanese remind us of the power of subtlety in the face of a craft beer market increasingly obsessed with high alcohol and even higher hopping rates. While a dry beer is hardly ever to be commended for its remarkable flavour qualities, it is a beer style thatworks well with dishes that would be easily trampled by anything more emphatic than, say, a Belgian-style wheat beer or a gently flavourful helles.

Lessons such as those gleaned from the English pub, the German beer hall, an American beer bar or a Japanese izakaya are fundamental, yet could perhaps be considered unsophisticated in comparison with modern culinary mores. Nonetheless, these tenets, constructed long before anyone paid attention to partnering this beer with that dish, are the building blocks of beer and food pairing.

The 'complement or contrast' guideline demonstrated so well by the Belgian and Czech experience for instance, is basic a rule of thumb for virtually all beverage and food pairing, be the drink wine or beer, whisky or cocktails. Sometimes 'cut' is added to the mix, meaning that the liquid should cut through the grease or spice of the dish, but in the case of beer that is managed by carbonation, as per the America example, and also, as we shall see later, hoppiness.

Subtlety as seen in the izakaya is an often-overlooked quality when it comes to beer and food pairings, just as the guidance provided by history whether in the pub, beerhall or elsewhere, can sometimes be ignored to the detriment of the gastronomic marriage.

Whether you are seeking to partner a beer with a complex pork dish – something German perhaps? – or creating an ideal pairing for a steak and ale pie – with a best bitter or pale ale? – these basics are bound to serve you well as a starting point. But the real excitement is yet to come.

A PINT AND A (PIZZA) PIE

QUITE POSSIBLY THE MOST ICONIC FOOD AND BEVERAGE PAIRING IN THE WORLD TODAY IS PIZZA AND BEER, THE DRIVING FORCE BEHIND INNUMERABLE PARTIES, A STAPLE OF TELEVISION SITCOMS AND SUBJECT OF AT LEAST ONE PUNK ROCK SONG. BUT AS MUCH AS WE ALL LOVE TO SETTLE DOWN WITH A FEW BREWS AND A LARGE 'ALL-DRESSED' PIZZA, WE TEND TO GIVE LITTLE ATTENTION TO HOW WE COMBINE THE TWO.

SO, THE NEXT TIME YOU GET THE URGE TO ORDER IN, OR ARE PAYING A VISIT TO ONE OF THE NEW AND EXPANDING BREED OF BEER-SAVVY PIZZA PARLOURS, CONSIDER THE FOLLOWING COMBINATIONS. YOU MIGHT JUST WIND UP LIKING PIZZA AND BEER EVEN MORE.

- **MARGHERITA:** VIENNA LAGER
- **PEPPERONI:** AMERICAN-STYLE PALE ALE
- **DIAVOLO (HOT SAUSAGE AND HOT PEPPERS):** AMERICAN-STYLE IPA
- **ALL-DRESSED:** AMERICAN-STYLE IPA, BUT A LOWER ALCOHOL VERSION (<6.5% ABV)
- **SAUSAGE:** RAUCHBIER (MÄRZEN OR LAGERBIER)
- **HAWAIIAN:** BROWN ALE OR NEW ZEALAND-STYLE PALE ALE
- **MEAT LOVER:** BOCK OR DOPPELBOCK
- **PRIMAVERA:** DUNKEL OR STEAM BEER
- **PESTO:** HELLES
- **WHITE PIZZA WITH CHICKEN:** HEFEWEIZEN

OPPOSITE Crate Brewery in London's newly fashionable East End district, is known for its delicious pizzas made on the premises in stone-bake ovens.

LEFT German Ayinger is one of those classic hefeweizens that not only quenches a thirst but successfully complements a wide range of Bavarian foods, most in some way incorporating pork.

BEER AND FOOD PAIRING

BEER AND FOOD PAIRING

BEER AND FOOD TODAY

IT IS HARD TO OVERSTATE THE DEGREE TO WHICH THE WORLD HAS CHANGED OVER THE COURSE OF THE LAST HALF-CENTURY. WHERE ONCE WE SCHEDULED LONG-DISTANCE TELEPHONE CALLS AND CAREFULLY MONITORED THEIR LENGTH LEST THEY BECOME TOO PRICEY, WE NOW COMMUNICATE ACROSS VAST DISTANCES AT THE DROP OF A HAT, FOR VERY LITTLE COST AT ALL, AND OFTEN WITH VIDEO ADDED. TRANSPORTATION HAS LIKEWISE SHRUNK THE GLOBE TO THE EXTENT THAT WE BOARD PLANES AS CASUALLY AS WE ONCE DID BUSES. AND PRODUCTS FROM AROUND THE WORLD ARE AS READILY AVAILABLE AS ITEMS CRAFTED UP THE ROAD OR FARMED NEARBY.

These advances have radically changed the modern world of beer and food, too. Where previously our cuisines were restricted by geography and immigration, now we find Thai restaurants in towns that have never seen a Thai resident, sushi bars thousands of kilometres/miles from the coast and North American cities boasting quantities of 'small plates' restaurants that rival the number of tapas bars in many Spanish cities.

As for beer, it's much the same story. During the 1970s, beer was exported by only the largest of the world's brewing companies, which by today's standards weren't actually that big at all. (By way of comparison, the world's largest brewing company in 1977 was Anheuser-Busch, with annual production of about 40 million hectolitres/1056 million gallons. Today's largest, Anheuser-Busch InBev, is responsible for over 10 times that amount.)

By the 1980s, things had begun to change, with smaller production brands from nations like Belgium and the Netherlands beginning to make international waves, and a new movement of what were then called microbreweries emulating the styles of other nations, whether that was a German-style lager brewed in London, an Irish-style stout produced in Toronto or a New York brewery making an English-style pale ale.

Fast forward two decades and things have changed again, with 'microbreweries' having morphed into 'craft breweries', largely because many had outgrown the 'micro' label, and a new generation of beer drinkers having grown accustomed to beers such as India pale ales, barley wines and Belgian-style everything. Paralleling the growth of international food, beer styles and the beers themselves, had by the first decade of the 21st century transcended national borders in a big way. It all adds up to a need for a re-examination of what we really mean by 'beer cuisine'.

TODAY, NOT ONLY DO WE HAVE TRULY INTERNATIONALIZED FOOD AND BEER, WE ARE ALSO FACED WITH A MORE DIVERSE BEER MARKET THAN EVER BEFORE, WITH PREVIOUSLY UNIMAGINED INGREDIENTS AND TECHNIQUES IN REGULAR DEPLOY; STYLES NATIVE TO EVERY CORNER OF THE GLOBE IMPORTED TO, OR EVEN PRODUCED AT THE BAR, SHOP OR BREWERY ACROSS TOWN; AND EXTINCT INDIGENOUS BEERS BROUGHT BACK TO LIFE BY ENTERPRISING BREWERS IN SEARCH OF THE NEXT BIG THING.

OPPOSITE ABOVE The Crown Tavern in London's Clerkenwell is an old Victorian pub updated in the 'craft beer' tradition and serving a wide variety of bar snacks alongside classic English pub food such as fish and chips, Sunday roasts and sausage and mash.

OPPOSITE BELOW The Craft Beer Company, with various bars in central and south London, serves traditional bar snacks including Scotch eggs and pork pies.

A 21ST-CENTURY MANIFESTO FOR BEER CUISINE

In previous times, beer cuisine or, more properly, *la cuisine à la bière* has been something principally associated with Belgium and parts of France, particularly the Nord-Pas-de-Calais. Typically, it involved beer being used as an ingredient, although for reasons of symmetry, if nothing else, the resulting dish was most often presented at the table with beer as an accompaniment.

In the second edition of his book, *Michael Jackson's Beer Companion*, the late beer maven observed that the notion of cooking with beer has a rich and storied history, citing recipes from the 1870s and culinary advocates as legendary as Auguste Escoffier himself. Further, he allows that in the mid 1990s, the notion of bringing beer to the kitchen has begun to spread to parts of Europe and the United States from its long-time home in Belgium and France, 'the geographical meeting point of the passions for good food and fine beer'.

Obviously, Jackson was right. In my office alone I have a collection of not one or two isolated books about cooking with beer, but shelves of volumes in languages from German to Danish to English and French, featuring recipes from brewpub cooks and Michelin-starred chefs. That such books and recipes exist is testament to the burgeoning popularity of *cuisine à la bière*. Even stronger than the global interest in cooking with beer is our collective fascination with partnering beer and food.

Despite the near ubiquity of artisanal breweries and the legions of passionate devotees who now monitor brewery special releases like young music fans following the every move of a cherished rock star, beer is still consigned to the

margins of cuisine with astonishing regularity. Chefs who pride themselves on coaxing every molecule of flavour out of a piece of turbot sing paeans of praise to industrial lager; restaurants with award-winning wine lists stock five or six very similar beers almost as an afterthought; and bars boasting 13-ingredient cocktails that take 10 minutes to mix offer only a trio of bland brews to pacify those who might not feel like sampling their Malaysia-inspired take on a margarita.

BEER AND FOOD DESTINATION

'LOGAN BROWN IN WELLINGTON, NEW ZEALAND, IS A LEADING RESTAURANT THAT OFFERS A SHORT BUT WELL-STYLED BEER LIST WHICH PRESENTS BEER IN A SOPHISTICATED MANNER, WITH AS MUCH FOCUS ON PRESENTATION AND GLASSWARE AS IS AFFORDED WINE.'

MATT KIRKEGAARD, EDITOR OF AUSTRALIAN BREWS NEWS AND 2014 AUSTRALIAN BEER WRITER OF THE YEAR

This is not good enough. Beer cuisine these days means more than just cooking with beer. It means having the beers that pair with the dishes on the menu, treating beer with the same sort of respect and consideration that is normally bestowed upon wine, and recognizing that in many instances the best partner for a given dish is a beer.

OPPOSITE ABOVE A barman bones up on his beer menu in the Falling Rock bar in Denver, Colorado.

OPPOSITE BELOW Thornbridge Brewery in Derbyshire, England has a stable of pubs, including a renowned bar at Sheffield railway station serving beer and food.

ABOVE Craft beer and tattoos are as ubiqutous as good beer and food pairings in may US and European beer bars.

Here we have the starting point of a new beer revolution. No longer should it be automatically assumed that everyone at a restaurant table will be drinking wine, and those who do desire a beer will not be content with a footnote of a beer list or a diminutive selection hastily recited by the server.

Mostly tasteless lagers churned out by brewing corporations that regularly give away more beer than a mid-sized craft brewery makes are fine if that is what you want, but not all of us want that.

What we want instead is the ability to choose beers that will pair well with the dishes we order, because, quite frankly, big brewery lagers don't pair well with much of anything. At the restaurant level, this requires having a beer list – that's a written list, not a few brands memorised by the server – and one which does more than just tick the boxes of what's easily obtainable or fashionable at the time. The list we want is one which involves the same sort of understanding and deliberation that today goes into the creation of a credible wine list, and most importantly also one which includes beers that harmonise well with the restaurant's cuisine.

It also means employing sommeliers and bartenders and servers who recognise that beer is the equal of wine and not an order to be frowned upon. At the very least, they need to have a basic understanding of all the major beer styles and be able to recommend as a minimum one pairing for every dish on the menu, if not three or four at different price points, as might be expected for wine. And when it comes time for the cheese course, let's all just stop pretending that wine is the most suitable partner and break out a few beers instead.

Because in the 21st century, this is what beer cuisine is about. Not ceding the stage automatically to wine, as was a given in days past, but taking it to the kitchen for creative beer-accented cuisine and bringing it to the table for gastronomically glorious beer and food pairings. Not clumsily pouring a refrigerator temperature barley wine into an iced, straight-sided glass, but presenting beer at the temperature and in the glassware at which it might be best enjoyed. And not dismissed as 'all the same', but celebrated for its variety of flavour and aromas and colours, and importantly, its ability to partner with any food.

This is not the same as declaring that from this day forward all beer and food pairing options must be presented and all matches must be perfect. That's never going to happen. But a little effort goes a long way and the days of staring down, say, a steak house menu replete with five selections of lager and two of pale ale should be behind us. They are not, but they should be.

Yes, it is indeed time for a beer and food revolution. As with any successful revolution, though, we're going to first need some guidelines.

OPPOSITE A glass of Dark Star Six Hop would pair well with any roast meat such as beef or lamb, in a casserole or a stew.

BELOW Mussels and wibtbier has long been a staple of Belgian cuisine.

STENE ISACSSON

STANDING UP FOR SWEDISH BEER

AKKURAT, STOCKHOLM, SWEDEN

IF YOU KNOW TWO THINGS ABOUT BEER IN STOCKHOLM, THEY ARE MOST LIKELY THE NAMES OF TWO WORLD-CLASS BEER DESTINATIONS LOCATED BUT A SHORT STROLL FROM ONE ANOTHER, OLIVER TWIST AND AKKURAT. IF YOU'RE LUCKY, YOU'LL GET TO VISIT ONE OR THE OTHER; STENE ISACSSON HAS MANAGED TO WORK IN BOTH, AND EVENTUALLY BECOME A PARTNER IN THE LATTER.

'I started working at Oliver Twist in 1993, moving to Akkurat when that opened in 1995,' he explains, 'When the opportunity to buy Akkurat presented itself in 2001, I and two colleagues took it!'

In the 20 years it has existed, Akkurat has been at the forefront of a developing Swedish craft beer scene, one which has thrived principally, Stene says, because of the influences it has absorbed from other countries.

'We still have to find our way back to our own roots, whatever they are,' he says, adding that for now, 'Anything that comes out of a brewery here will almost certainly be a style from another region or a well-known style with a twist to it. In a way it feels almost like we are still a young country'.

When I express surprise that the well-known Nordic Cuisine movement has not yet had a beery offshoot, Stene counters that some experiments are underway, citing in particular Närke Kulturbryggeri and the beers they are flavouring with pine shoots and old Swedish hop varieties, now only growing in the wild, plus a few breweries now using Swedish or Scandinavian grains. Still, he admits, the progress is slow and the interest not terribly high.

'WE STILL HAVE A BIT TO GO BEFORE FINDING THE AUTHENTIC SCANDINAVIAN FLAVOURS IN BOTH BEER AND FOOD,' HE OFFERS, 'AND EVEN LONGER BEFORE THEY BECOME CLASSICS THAT YOU CAN FIND IN ANY RESTAURANT'.

There is, however, one area in which the Swedish kitchen certainly does excel, and that is in smoked fish. It is not only something Akkurat does very well, but also according to Stene an area that offers great possibilities for food and beer pairing.

'Something that's very important when pairing food and beer is the little flavour element added to the dish' he says, "For example, the smoked herring we have on the menu now is quite a complicated dish, with the herring itself being quite fatty and smoky, the dark soda bread that has been fried in butter, the pickled onions and the dill, and then the potato crème and poached quail egg that bind all the flavours together. So there are actually a bunch of different ways you can go'.

With that, he rhymes off a brown ale as a possible flavour hook for the bread, a hoppy but not aggressive pilsner that cuts through the fattiness of the fish, and a stout to pick up on the saltiness and smokiness of the dish. In general, however, and without taking heed of the other flavours involved, he points to a smoked malt beer like a rauchbier or smoked porter as a foil to smoked fish, 'something balanced and easy yet still powerful enough to not be overrun by the food.' Alternately, he observes that there is always the possibility of a well-made lager.

'We are still a lager country,' he notes, 'That has been our beer style for so long that we've almost forgotten about the fact that we used to drink a lot of porters back in the day but still, I think most of our traditional dishes match perfectly with a well-crafted lager beer'.

OPPOSITE Stene Isaacson is an influential member of the craft beer and food movement in his native Sweden, where he is joint owner of Akkurat, a Stockholm beer-cellar destination.

THE ESSENTIALS OF BEER AND FOOD PAIRING

Food and drink professionals often talk about the 'three Cs' of beverage pairing – Complement, Contrast and Cut, the last two of which are really two sides of the same coin, but more about that later. To this dynamic and very useful trio of guiding principles I would add one other, Context. More about that later, too, but for now let's look at the big three.

COMPLEMENTARY PAIRINGS

By far the simplest way in which to marry food with any beverage, be it beer, wine, cocktail, spirit or Indian lassi, is through a complementary relationship. And what this means is exactly as simple as it sounds, although with a qualification or two.

The Collins English Dictionary defines 'complement' as "one of two parts that make up a whole or complete each other" and 'complementary' as "forming a satisfactory or balanced whole". In other words, in literary terms, a complementary food and beer pairing is one in which the two parts balance each other and make up something greater than the sum of their individual parts.

More practically, a food and beer pairing that is complementary is one in which the two flavours will share a common bond of aroma and flavour. So a sweet and fruity dessert, for example, would find an easy complement in a beer that is flavoured with the same fruits, while a bowl of mixed nuts will be nicely accompanied by a brown ale with a dry and notably nutty character.

BEER AND FOOD DESTINATION

'AT BIRCH & BARLEY IN WASHINGTON DC, THEY HAVE A DIVERSE MENU OF FOODS AND A WIDE RANGE OF DRAUGHT BEERS, WITH ALL AVAILABLE IN 120ML (4 FL OZ) POURS – PERFECT FOR MATCHING A COURSE, OR FOR SELECTING A COUPLE OF BEERS TO TRY WITH A COURSE.'

RAY DANIELS, FOUNDER AND DIRECTOR OF THE CICERONE CERTIFICATION PROGRAM

Obvious problems arise when we get into foods like grilled steak or pork sausage, since it's pretty difficult to find steak- or sausage-flavoured beer. (Even as I type these words, I fear that some enterprising craft brewer has already begun work on developing a sirloin stock ale.) And so we expand the complementary relationship to deal with generalities rather than specifics, acknowledging that a steak has sweet notes from the meat, a metallic tang from the blood and charred or smoky notes from the caramelisation of fats on the grill, and so would find a complementary relationship with a rich brown ale or porter boasting similar flavour elements.

ABOVE For a successful complementary pairing for skewered grilled prawns, match them to a Vienna lager or pilsner.

OPPOSITE At The Boater pub in Bath, owned by the UK brewer Fuller's, classic pub food is complemented by a full range of Fuller's beer and guest ales.

Similarly, a pork sausage might have herbal notes from the meat mixture, a mouth-filling quality derived from the fattiness of the pork and perhaps a bit of spiciness, as well, leading us to a round, full and herbal-spicy bock or doppelbock.

The more you experiment with complementary relationships, the more obvious they appear, since eating and drinking are essentially emotional experiences felt as a whole, rather than as individual components. The cake that makes you swoon, for instance, is not being tasted as vanilla and sugar in the cake, sweet butter and darkly bitter chocolate in the icing, plus a fruity note of cherries on top, but rather, as CAKE!

Extend that tasting analogy one step further and food and beer, when expertly partnered, can become as one, completing each other and forming a single, seamless flavour experience. So no longer are you chewing one thing, a steak or sausage or piece of cake, and drinking another, a brown ale or bock or Scotch ale, but instead you are revelling in STEAKBROWNALE or SAUSAGEBOCK or CAKESCOTCHALE. In other words, to return to the dictionary, you have taken two parts and made a whole of them.

CONTRAST AND CUT IN PAIRING

Developing successful contrasting relationships in food and beer is more complicated than forging complementary ones, but when the right pairing is reached, it can be highly rewarding. There are a couple of approaches that work.

The most basic form of contrast is the pairing of foods and beers of opposite weights, so a rich and filling dish could be partnered with a more simple, mild-mannered brew or, more rarely, a food that is light in character is matched to a robust beer. Let's begin with the former.

Eating is a stomach-filling experience. That is, after all, the whole point of the exercise, since food equals nutrition and all animals require nutrients in order to survive. That said, it is also true that some foods are more filling than others: hearty meat stews compared to poached whitefish, for instance, or an ice cream sundae relative to a sliced pear. With such gut-busting dishes, complementary beers, higher alcohol porters or strong dark ales with the stew, for example, can feel a bit like piling weight upon weight. A contrasting beer, on the other hand, offers the ideal respite.

Returning to our stew, imagine instead of weighty dark ales, (which are psychologically more substantial than they are in reality, since we often perceive darker beverages as being bigger and fuller than their light-hued kin) a lighter-bodied standard bitter, with a lower calorie count due to its weaker strength and a dryness that refreshes between forkfuls. Or think of the banana split teamed with a slightly sweetish hefeweizen boasting a commonality in the form of the banana-like esters such beers tend to present, alongside a light and quenching nature.

The flip side of this equation, when a bigger brew pairs with a lightly flavourful food, is perhaps best illustrated through the centuries-old partnership of black beers and the fruits of the sea, particularly oysters.

Said to have been born on the bar tops of Victorian London pubs, porter or stout with oysters is considered one of the world's most long-standing pairings, and it is one which works despite the exquisitely nuanced flavour of the molluscs. The key, according to my extensive experience, resides in the briny nature of the oyster 'liquor,' or the sea water-accented liquid contained in the shell, which plays off the ever-so-slightly saline flavours that tend to manifest themselves in beer when roasted barley or black malts are present. Aside from the salty flavour hook, porters and stouts have generally dry to off-dry roasty flavours that provide a juxtaposition to sweet raw oysters.

The pairing works equally as well with clams, winkles, cockles and some preparations of crab and lobster, largely for the same reason. One of my most memorable food and beer experiences revolved around a pot full of steamed clams and several pints of porter, all enjoyed in the open air on a cool but gloriously sunny day in Portland, Oregon.

The other element of contrast intersects with the notion of the cut and involves exclusively bold flavours. Here an apt illustration is provided by the classically indulgent pasta dish, fettuccine Alfredo. Although rich with cream, butter and cheese, the Alfredo character is less that of a dense and heavy dish (when well made, it can seem almost light) and more like one that coats the mouth with flavourful oils. Adding to this character with a round and malty ale would only add to the sweetness of the fats, doing nothing to invigorate the palate between bites. A crisp pilsner or pale ale however would not only offer a tasty and refreshing contrast, but would also cut through the fat with effervescence and hoppiness.

Similarly, a thick cream soup can be contrasted and cut by a hoppy pilsner or kölsch and a Boston clam chowder by a hoppy porter, while a triple cream cheese can welcome a dry stout, and a piece of braised pork belly is sublime with its fat and salt tamed by a bubbly hefeweizen or crisp helles.

OPPOSITE A crispy jalapeño hot dog teamed with Brewdog's Punk IPA is a great example of a 'contrast and cut' beer and food pairing.

PAIRING AND CONTEXT

Back in the day, if you wanted to experience what it was like to combine, say, Westmalle Tripel and in-season white asparagus, you had two choices: 1) You travelled to Belgium; or 2) You didn't experience it. This was not necessarily such a bad thing.

Today, of course, Westmalle Tripel is fairly widely exported and white asparagus is no longer the limited availability delicacy it once was, so combining the two is not that difficult. In fact, as I sit in my office in Toronto on a February afternoon, I know that I could walk two blocks up the road to buy some Tripel before venturing a bit further to get some hothouse-farmed white asparagus and be enjoying the combination by dinnertime.

What would be missing from my mid-winter experience would be context, and in a world where the international trade in beer is at an all-time high and foodstuffs have long since lost their sense of 'specialness', or at very least are losing it fast, that can make a world of difference.

Take, for example, a Belgian adventure I had in the late 1990s, after the world had been clued in to the beauty of beers from 'Het Bierland' but before those beers were as widely exported as they are today. The brewery in question was what is perhaps the most revered and certainly the most cloistered of all the Belgian Trappist abbey breweries, Westvleteren, and the location was the café that operates immediately opposite the monastery, In de Vrede.

Following an impromptu visit to the abbey – such things were still possible back then, before the website ratebeer.com declared Westvleteren 12 to be the best beer in the world and drew the brewery very reluctantly into the international spotlight – my companion and I had repaired to the café for lunch and a couple of bottles of beer. Our meal was simple, the beer was delicious, and we were ready to depart when a sudden urge compelled me to order for dessert the *coupe In de Vrede,* an ice cream made with the Westvleteren beer, and a bottle of the Westvleteren 12.

Even now, almost two decades later, I can remember the experience as one of the finest beer and food pairings I have ever enjoyed. The ice cream was sublime and the beer expressed itself in every bit of its robust, malt-filled glory, combining with the dessert to form a deliriously delicious whole. Given that In de Vrede is a fairly simple café – I have returned since to confirm this fact – and I recall nothing else from that or subsequent meals as being terribly special, in retrospect I doubt that my experience was truly as transformative as it seems in my memory. But such is the power of context.

Such contextual pleasures exist still, thank goodness, even in the fast-paced, jet-setting, ever-connected world in which we live today. Kölsch from Cologne, Germany, is widely available bottled or canned, and the style is oft-imitated, but none will taste the same as a *stange,* or traditional cylindrical glass, of fresh beer enjoyed with the cheese and bread snack known as *halve hahn* in the shadow of Köln cathedral. The Chinese beer Tsingtao is now one of the world's best-sellers, but no bottle brought around the world will compare with a plastic bag growler filled at the brewery with the unpasteurised and unfiltered version, perhaps to be sipped alongside a plate of *qingdao guotie,* or the local pot stickers. And while various fried chicken parts are sold in bars, pubs and cafés the world over, nothing can quite compare to the Brazilian chicken thigh speciality, *coxinha,* partnered with a fresh draught Colorado Indica IPA at the São Paulo bar, FrangÓ.

OPPOSITE ABOVE The three grains using in the brewing of Tripel Karmeliet – barley, wheat and oats – produce a malt complexity that is suitable for pairing with a variety of food, notably white asparagus.

OPPOSITE BELOW Context can be all important for a memorable beer and food pairing. Eating fish on the coast accompanied by a local witbier is bound to be a better experience than the same combination consumed in the centre of a city.

If beer has one secret weapon when it comes to forming partnerships with food, it is the humble hop.

The source of innumerable aromas and flavours, hops are of course also the primary supplier of bitterness to beer, that essential quality which prevents the sweetness of residual malt sugars from becoming cloying, and adds layers of depth and complexity. And when it comes to pairing with food, as acidity is to wine, more or less, hoppiness is to beer.

For those more familiar with pairing wine and food than they are beer and food, the equation is relatively simple: In situations when you would ordinarily reach for a wine of high acidity, look instead to a beer of significant hoppiness. For the rest of us, a few more details are in order.

BEER AND FOOD DESTINATION

'RESTOBIÈRES IN BRUSSELS WAS A WONDERFUL EXPERIENCE WHICH I CHERISH, AND HOPE TO EXPERIENCE AGAIN. IT WAS ABOUT THE BEER, THE FOOD, THE PEOPLE I WAS WITH, THE HOSPITALITY OF THE OWNER, AND HIS ENTERTAINMENT.'

LUKE NICHOLAS, OWNER OF EPIC BREWING, NEW ZEALAND

All wines have acidity, just like all beers have hoppiness, even when they don't seem to taste at all bitter. (This is not to discount the historic category of beer known as *gruit*, which is brewed with herbs rather than hops, but such beers are commercially produced in tiny numbers.) The key in both cases is the degree of hoppiness or acidity.

Typical areas where higher acidity wines shine include fatty, oily, salty and spicy foods, although the last is a bit of a point of contention among some sommeliers. These are also areas where hoppier beers shine, and for mostly the same reasons acidic wines work so well.

Where fats and oils are concerned, wine's acidity can help cut through the grease and refresh the palate between bites, just as a beer's hoppiness will accomplish the same task. Where salt is concerned, bitterness can help balance the salt by moderating one elemental flavour with another, pushing aside the saltiness until the next bite. In both such

instances, beer has the added bonus of carbonation, which helps to strip the palate of a build-up of fat and salt.

Spicy foods and acidic wines are recommended by some and maligned by others, just as there are those who think hoppiness and spicy heat create too many high flavour points when combined. Personally, I believe that hops have a tremendous ability to moderate the heat while still maintaining the taste of the pepper, softening the 'pain factor' but not freezing out the flavour as would the stereotypical ice-cold light lager. Add a little sweetness into the equation, as with a balanced double IPA, and you have two moderating effects working as one.

If bitterness were all hops brought to the beer-pairing party, that would certainly suffice – after all, the parallel role played by acidity in wine is enough that oenologists drone on at length about the levels of acidity in certain wines. But hoppiness is about much more than just bitterness; it's nuttiness and citrussy notes and tropical fruitiness and herbal aromas and so very much more. When any of these flavours is combined with the general fat-oil-salt-spice equation, it allows for a partnership that doesn't simply 'work,' as one often hears about wine in such situations, but one that might shine most gloriously.

A good way in which to illustrate the food pairing fortitude of hoppy beers is to try a malty beer and a hoppy one alongside typical bar room fare such as pretzels (salty), a hamburger (fatty) or jalapeño-topped nachos (spicy). What you are most likely to find is that the malty beer loses lustre in the face of the salt, grows flabby when combined with fat and is diminished in body by the spicy assault of the hot peppers, while in each instance the hoppy beer stands up to and combines well with the highly-charged nature of the foods.

OPPOSITE ABOVE Whether jalapeño-topped or not, the salty and fatty quality of nachos suit them to hoppy beers from pilsners to pale ales and IPAs.

OPPOSITE BELOW When choooosing a beer to go with or fatty, salty and spicy foods, look out for a hoppy one.

SUSANNE HECHT
WEISSBIER EVANGELIST

KELHEIM, GERMANY

GROWING UP NEAR A BREWERY IS NOT NECESSARILY A TICKET TO A JOB IN THE BEER BUSINESS, ESPECIALLY WHEN YOU DON'T EVEN PARTICULARLY LIKE BEER, BUT FOR SUSANNE HECHT, THAT'S THE WAY IT WORKED OUT.

Living near the G. Schneider & Sohn weissbier brewery in Kelheim, Germany, it seemed only natural for Susanne to apply for part-time work with the company while she was growing up and perusing studies close to home. It was a six month post-grad term as brewery head Georg Schneider's assistant that really immersed her into the world of beer, though that position turned rather unexpectedly into a longer term role, when Schneider was asked whether she would consider taking on the suddenly vacant role of head of export sales.

Susanne admits that her chief qualification for the job at the time was her ability to speak English, but with the support of the senior Schneider and a network of international customers she describes as 'very helpful', plus a love of travel, she soon found herself settling into the job. In the years since, she has developed not only an obvious passion for beer, but also a keen interest in beer and food pairing and other aspects of beer enjoyment, a curiosity that led her to take the beer sommelier course offered by the German brewing school Doemens in 2008.

Not that is has been easy convincing Germans of the merits of different ways in which to enjoy beer. 'Beer here has for so long been a part of people's normal lives that they don't really think about it, they just want a thirst quencher', she says, 'So when we started hosting beer dinners, even our staff didn't understand why we weren't serving a half-litre of every beer, why we were using wine glasses and such'.

Still, she has soldiered on, aided, she says, by the ease with which weissbier pairs with food. 'Because of the high carbonation, you can use weissbier to cleanse the palate when you have fats or oily foods', she advises, 'And of course there are the natural pairings of the region, like roast pork or pretty much anything that is roasted, especially with the Schneider Weiss Unser Original'.

It doesn't take long for the jet-setting Saleswoman to start expanding on many other food pairings for Schneider beers, whether it's as simple and basic as a pizza paired with the Original, again using the beer's ample carbonation as a palate cleanser, or as involved as a creamy, Black Forest cake-based dessert she once had paired with Aventinus at a small restaurant in the Brazilian city of Blumenau.

'I ALSO LIKE TO PRESENT BEER AND CHOCOLATE PAIRINGS BECAUSE IT ATTRACTS WOMEN', SUSANNE ADDS, 'MILK CHOCOLATE WITH CARAMELIZED MACADAMIA NUTS PAIRED WITH THE ORIGINAL IS A FAVOURITE BECAUSE YOU HAVE THE SWEETNESS AND NUTTINESS, PLUS THE MOUTH-FILLING NATURE OF THE CHOCOLATE, THAT BRINGS OUT THE BEST IN THE BEER'.

Ask for her favourite pairing of all, however, and Susanne surprises with a partnership that is decidedly unBavarian in form: 'For me, it is an Indian curry with the Hopfenweiss'. she says, 'I find that really spicy curries can be too hot for me, but the Hopfenweiss makes the spice so much more pleasant. I really enjoy that'.

OPPOSITE ABOVE Crates of Schneider weiss beer are exported all over the world. The beer is a classic of its kind.

OPPOSITE BELOW LEFT In Munich the Weisses brauhaus, once the Schneider brewery, is a now a popular food and drink destination.

OPPOSITE BELOW RIGHT Susanne Hecht has long been hosting beer dinners at the Schneider Weiss Brewery in Kelheim, Germany.

THE SWEETNESS FACTOR

The yin to beer's hoppy yang is, of course, its malty sweetness. It is the backbone on which bitterness is hung in hoppy styles such as IPA and Imperial stout and the source of depth, richness and the rich mosaic of flavours in malt-driven beers like doppelbock and Scotch ale. It is also the quality that makes certain malt-forward styles, dubbel and bock, for example, the remarkably versatile and food-friendly beers that they are.

The key to that second point is the diversity of flavours that emanate from the almost infinite ways in which different malts may be combined in a beer, from the simple and straight-forward sweet grain of a pale malt helles or pilsner to the complex dark fruit, spice and cocoa or even tanned leather notes of a five or six malt barley wine. Although such flavour notes lend themselves to partnering with a wide array of different foods, there are occasions when a cautious approach with respect to a beer's sweetness is recommended, such as when it comes to time for dessert.

Except when there are distinctly complementary flavours to be built upon, a nutty pale ale with a nutty dessert, for example, or when chocolate is involved, it is always recommended that the sweetness of a beer roughly match or even exceed the sweetness of the dessert being paired. The reasoning behind this has to do with the interaction of flavours and how the palate perceives sugar.

WHEN YOU EAT OR DRINK SOMETHING SOUR OR BITTER AND THEN FOLLOW IT WITH SOMETHING SWEET, THE SWEETNESS IS GOING TO SEEM EXAGGERATED IN RELATIVE TERMS. CONVERSELY, WHEN A SOUR OR BITTER FOOD OR BEVERAGE FOLLOWS SOMETHING SWEET, IT WILL TASTE MORE SOUR OR BITTER. IT'S SIMPLE FLAVOUR RELATIVITY.

So if you were to pair, say, an ordinary blonde ale, not too sweet and not too hoppy, with a piece of sweet cake, that beer would wind up tasting relatively bitter, if not somewhat dull, while the cake would taste sweeter and more like a sugar assault. Partner in a Scotch ale, a strong and sweet Belgian-style spiced ale or a doppelbock, on the other hand, and the sweetness of both cake and beer will balance out in a meeting of equals rather than opposites.

This relationship is something that should also be kept in mind when pairing beers with foods that have undergone a Maillard reaction during cooking. (Sometimes called 'the beginning of caramelisation', the Maillard reaction involves the rearranging of sugars and amino acids in foods cooked at high temperature. It can result in the appearance of sweeter flavours, although this is not always the case.) When browning occurs during the cooking process, a sure sign of Maillard, care should be taken to balance the sweetness with that of the chosen beer.

OPPOSITE ABOVE Chocolate pudding, vanilla ice cream and spun sugar features on the menu of Fuller's pubs in the UK.

OPPOSITE BELOW Sticky toffee pudding is a staple pudding that partners well with a Scotch ale or a sweet, spiced ale.

ABOVE White chocolate and ice cream is a sublime combination that works well accompanied by a sweet and strong golden ale.

SRIRAM AYLUR

MICHELIN-STARRED BEER AFICIONADO

QUILON RESTAURANT, LONDON, ENGLAND

WHEN MOST PEOPLE THINK ABOUT BEER AND INDIAN FOOD, THE PAIRING THAT COMES TO MIND IS A SPICY CURRY AND AN ICE-COLD LAGER. THOSE PEOPLE HAVE NOT EATEN AT CHEF SRIRAM AYLUR'S ESTEEMED TEMPLE OF GASTRONOMY, QUILON.

Having firmly established himself as one of India's best chefs in the last decade of the 20th century, Sriram came to London to open Quilon in 1999 and in so doing brought an approach to his native cuisine quite different to what was the widely accepted norm in the English capital at the time. Instead of the fiery vindaloos and other dishes so popular in London curry houses, he offered the lighter, more delicate and complex cuisine of the coastal southwest region of India, in short order earning widespread acclaim and, eventually, a Michelin star for his efforts.

He also brought an appreciation of beer.

'Personally, beer is one of my favourite drinks,' the chef says, 'So it seemed right to serve a selection in the restaurant, which we started doing about ten or eleven years ago. After that, it just made sense that we would offer the pairings'.

The 'pairings' Sriram refers to are two set menus, one of five courses and the other of eight, both of which partner each dish with a specific beer. Not exactly something generally seen in your average Indian restaurant, much less a Michelin-starred one.

'Part of our motivation was that we wanted to show people that beer has its own styles, its own character, and that it can be matched to the food just like wine', the chef says, adding with refreshing candour that, 'The only things our guests walk out with are the experience and the bill, so it is up to us to make sure that the experience is interesting and memorable. Beer pairings help us do that'.

While they are happy to serve wine with your meal at Quilon, Sriram sees a logic in offering beer at the restaurant, although it's not the 'beer and Indian food' or even the 'curry and IPA' logic you might expect.

'England is a beer country', he notes, 'In France, which is a wine country, obviously, it makes sense to pair your food with wine, so in the UK it makes sense to pair with beer'.

Asked for hints on how he goes about making his beer selections, Sriram displays the practical, flavour-focussed demeanor of a truly great chef.

'When we make the pairings, there are a few things we keep in mind' he explains, 'obviously balance is one of them and we want to make sure that the beer is not overpowering the food, and we also look at the flavours to find complementary relationships. In the end, the dishes will dictate the beers'.

More specifically, Sriram finds that lighter, floral beers – such as the wheat beers, lagers and not-too-hoppy ales that dominate Quilon's list – partner best with the delicacy of his cuisine. 'That said, however, we do find that IPAs pair very well with tandoori dishes', the chef adds.

Arguing that the first rule of any beverage and food pairing should be to 'drink what you like and enjoy', Sriram is extremely reluctant to pass judgement on any preferred partnership of beer and food, even the clichéd frosty cold, light-bodied lager with a plate of highly spiced curry. Even so, he does add a note of caution for pairings that involve his restaurant's style of cuisine.

'The lightness of the food makes beer pairing quite interesting,' he says, 'Because the flavours are subtle, you need to be careful with what beers you choose since some of the bigger and bolder ones can actually spoil the experience'.

OPPOSITE Sriram Aylur is a Michelin-starred chef who uses his appreciation of beer to create pairings that work with the Indian food he prepares at his award-winning restaurant, Quilon, in London.

COOKING WITH BEER

COOKING WITH BEER

BEER AND FOOD TODAY

IF YOU DRINK BEER AND YOU COOK, EVEN OCCASIONALLY, CHANCES ARE HIGH THAT YOU HAVE AT SOME POINT USED BEER IN THE KITCHEN. FOR THERE IS A TRUTH BEHIND THE TONGUE-IN-CHEEK FRIDGE MAGNET THAT DECLARES 'I LOVE COOKING WITH BEER, AND SOMETIMES I EVEN PUT IT IN THE FOOD!' AND THAT TRUTH IS THAT OCCASIONALLY A DISH WILL CALL FOR THE ADDITION OF SOME LIQUID, AND BEER WILL SIMPLY SEEM LIKE THE SIMPLEST SOLUTION AT HAND.

I've certainly done it. A slow simmering stew looks like it could use a bit more stock, but there is a glass of brown ale already nearby so the pot gets some of that instead. A four-alarm chilli that's been simmering for hours looks like it might be getting a bit on the dry side, so in goes some Vienna lager. Even something as simple as deglazing a pan with a splash or two of stout also counts.

THE TRUTH IS, COOKING WITH BEER REALLY IS THAT EASY. THE BROWN ALE IS GOING TO ADD CARAMELLY FLAVOURS TO THE STEW, JUST AS THE MALTY CHARACTER OF THE LAGER WILL CONTRIBUTE A TOUCH OF SWEETNESS TO THE HELP BALANCE THE SPICINESS OF THE CHILLI. AND WHILE IT MIGHT BE A BIT OF A STRETCH, THE RESIDUAL SUGARS FROM THE STOUT ARE GOING TO ADD A CARAMELIZING EFFECT TO WHATEVER BITS AND PIECES ARE BEING PULLED OFF THE DEGLAZED PAN.

be packed with great recipes, somehow overlook the basic dos and don'ts of bringing beer into the kitchen, ignoring the distinct probability that someone with sufficient interest in beer cuisine that they would buy a beer cookbook might also be the type of person to freestyle a beer-inclusive recipe on their own.

This chapter is devoted to helping you navigate the multitude of ways to bring beer into your food, without winding up with a piece of poached fish that tastes like it had spent its final days in a lake of pale ale, or a chocolate cake that boasts a flavour residing somewhere between bitter coffee and fireplace embers.

Still, as significant as these almost effortless applications may be, they are merely the tip of quite a grand iceberg of culinary opportunity where beer is concerned. Given the dramatic range of flavours and aromas available in beer, from tart to sweet, citrussy to vanilla-soaked, spicy to profoundly bitter, the surprising thing isn't that beer gets used in the kitchen, it's that it isn't employed more often.

There are indeed hundreds of uses for beer in cooking, and almost as many potential *faux pax* as well. Yet for some reason, many beer-oriented cookbooks, though they might

ABOVE Pork pies and a glass of best bitter? Don't mind if I do!

OPPOSITE A splash or two of witbier can liven up a cucumber salad, helping create a refreshing companion to a grilled sandwich.

SIMPLE MARINATING OR BRINING

Without question one of the most straightforward ways in which to bring beer to the kitchen is as a marinade. As Harold McGee notes in his landmark book, *On Food and Cooking*, marinades were originally used primarily to slow spoilage of the meat and add flavour, whereas today they are employed more for that second function, plus perhaps the addition of moisture to the meat being marinated.

CLASSIC MARINADES HAVE ACIDS IN THEM, WHICH HELPS INCREASE THE MEAT'S ABILITY TO RETAIN MOISTURE BY BREAKING DOWN MUSCLE TISSUE, AND IT IS CERTAINLY NOT A BAD IDEA TO MIX A LITTLE VINEGAR INTO YOUR BEER MARINADE FOR THAT EXPRESS PURPOSE.

Bear in mind, however, that very hoppy beers will have a similar, if lesser effect, to the point that soft meats like seafood can literally fall apart when marinated or poached in a particularly hoppy beer.

(Very hoppy beers are best used cautiously where marinades are concerned for another reason. If the marinated meat is to receive a long slow cooking, as many marinated meats do, the intensity of the concentrated hoppiness in even a small amount of absorbed beer can contribute unwanted bitterness.)

One good plan for choosing an ale or lager to use in a marinade is to match intensity of the beer with that of the meat. So for a shrimp marinade, select a beer that is light and definitely not hoppy, such as a Belgian style wheat beer, a helles or a fruity golden ale. Conversely, when marinating beef, you'll want to pick something more rich and full-bodied, like a porter or brown ale or sweet stout, and if marinating a cut that won't spend too much time cooking, such as a rib steak for grilling, try a moderately bitter or spicy ale to add an interesting flavour note to the meat.

It continues on the intensity scale: chicken and turkey will welcome wheat beers, light ales such as milds or golden ales; pork cuts can handle a bit more robustness, perhaps a bock or altbier; and game meats can usually take a variety of intense flavours, from gueuze lambics – rabbit marinated and cooked in gueuze is a Flemish classic – to pale ales for venison and bison. And don't forget that if the meat will generally welcome fruit as an accompaniment at the table, such a lamb and duck, it will generally also fare well in a fruit beer-based marinade.

Brining is a cooking method undergoing a bit of a renaissance these days, especially where turkey is involved, but a surprising number of people don't seem to quite comprehend the science behind the process. Without getting into too much detail, a brine simply pulls some of the liquid content out of a piece of meat and replaces it with an excess amount of a different liquid, so that the meat actually emerges from the brine more moist than it was originally. And since cooking always extracts moisture from meat, starting with more means ending up with a juicier, tastier cut.

For your brine, then, you could simply use water and sugar and salt, or you could go one step further and have that moisture absorbance be something quite tasty, like beer. The key, as with marinating, is to stay away from overly bitter beers and look for flavours that are harmonious with the meat being brined, such as a clove-accented hefeweizen for a ham, for instance.

OPPOSITE Beef marinated in beer takes on a rich, malty flavour the longer you leave it.

Since beer is mostly water, there is a temptation for some people to consider it as a steaming liquid, but don't. The fact is that the flavour elements in beer form a very, very small percentage of the overall liquid composition and simply won't play much of a role in flavouring what is being steamed, if indeed it contributes anything at all.

What you can do with steamed vegetables and dumplings instead, however, is to add some beer influence in the form of a sauce or dipping liquid for use after the cooking is done. Simply take some malty and spicy beer and reduce it in a saucepan to intensify its flavours, adjusting as necessary with extra spices, perhaps a little honey or mustard, and serve. It's a great way to add a beery element to any suitable dish, not just steamed foods.

The exception to the steaming rule is, of course, steamed seafood. Beer-steamed mussels and, to a lesser degree, clams are served all over the world now, and for very good reason, since they are relatively inexpensive to buy, easy to prepare and can be absolutely delicious. The key, however, is that the beer is less of a flavour in the actual shellfish than it is a component of a wonderful sauce that gets scooped up in the shell, sometimes slurped from a spoon and definitely soaked into fresh bread at the table.

STEWING AND SAUCING DISHES, ON THE OTHER HAND, ARE PRIME OCCASIONS FOR THE USE OF BEER, AND UNDER THE RIGHT CIRCUMSTANCES ARE EVEN SUITABLE PLACES FOR HOPPY BEERS.

By their very definition, stews call for the application of generous amounts of liquid. In many cases, recipes will call for beef or vegetable or some other stock, or even just plain water, and that is likely just fine for the dish being cooked. But if mere water is a good medium for, say, a lamb stew, imagine how much better it would be if half that liquid was replaced with an abbey-style dubbel. Or if a tomato-vegetable ragout had added, in place of vegetable stock, a mix of stock and Vienna lager. Or if a beef carbonade was cooked with...oh, wait, carbonade already is cooked in beer! (As it is in Alain Fayt's wonderful version on page 178).

Further, the beers used don't need to be uniformly malty, since hop oils will intensify significantly only if the boiling point is reached. A stew kept at a slow simmer, then, will welcome readily a pale ale or IPA, provided that it boasts the right flavours for the job, and especially so if the dish is spicy or features resinous herbal flavours that will bond with the taste of the hops.

A similar hoppy-spicy relationship will hold when a sauce is being developed for something like a curry or a spicy pasta dish, the former of which can often benefit from a pale ale or IPA made with citrusy American hops. Since these hop flavours can help juice up the character of such sauces, however, it is best to add them towards the end of the cooking, so that the hop flavour stays fresh and the bitterness is not allowed to intensify.

When maltier beers are put to use in sauces, it can be beneficial to reduce them first, eliminating some of the water and intensifying the sweet flavours. Just be sure to taste them as they reduce, so as to avoid the somewhat acrid taste that can affect an over-reduced beer.

For malty beers and stews, again, make sure that the beer you are choosing bears the same sort of flavour weight as the dish you are cooking. A lamb stew made with Scotch ale could yield a delicious result, for instance, but it is far less likely that a seafood stew cooked with the same beer would yield the same effect.

OPPOSITE In a stew, replace half the required liquid with a beer and wait for the wonderful flavours to emerge.

MAIN DISHES

Grab a cookbook, any cookbook. Now open it up to a random main course recipe and look at the cooking technique. Whatever it is, be it grilling or sautéing, stewing or braising, there is certainly a way to work beer into the ingredients, usually to quite a positive effect.

Let's begin with grilling, since the image of the barbecue cook manning the grill with a spatula or set of tongs in one hand and a beer in the other is about as iconic a beer-and-cooking picture as you'll ever see. And let's also start with what a lot of people do wrong.

ONE OF THE MISCONCEPTIONS THAT BEDEVILS OTHERWISE WELL-INTENTIONED GRILL-HANDS IS THAT A SPLASH OF BEER ON THE FOOD WHILE IT'S COOKING IS IN SOME WAY BASTING THE MEAT TO ITS BENEFIT. IT IS NOT.

Since the alcohol in beer is not high enough to cause a flare from the grill, as would happen if you dribbled a little bourbon over the meat, for instance, the sugars contained in the beer won't caramelize and the net effect will be only a loss of beer from your glass. Rather than adding flavours to the meat, all that flow of beer is really doing is splashing on to the charcoal, wood or gas fire below, lowering the cooking temperature of the fire and therefore exerting a negative rather than a positive effect on the grilling process.

Instead, try marinating your ingredients before taking them to the grill, as was explained earlier in this chapter, or if you're cooking burgers you can take a trick from the kitchen of beerbistro, the Toronto beer cuisine restaurant I helped get started back in the early years of this century.

The idea was one conceived by executive chef and beerbistro co-founder Brian Morin, who, along with people like Sean Paxton and Lucy Saunders, has been the source of much of my cooking with beer knowledge. Rather than trying to use the beer at the grill, Brian elected to work it into the mix beforehand by adding a handful of breadcrumbs and some malty ale to the burger meat mixture.

Since the bread will absorb the beer, the sugars from the beer are left in the meat to caramelize on the grill and produce more flavour and a tasty crust around the outside of the meat. It's a technique that can be used for any sort of burger, from beef to turkey to seafood, but again, avoid hoppy beers unless you're interested in a very bitter burger.

OPPOSITE Brining chicken in beer prior to cooking will yield a moister, more flavourful bird.

ABOVE LEFT Set a celebratory tone with beer at the table, as well as in the food.

ABOVE RIGHT For burgers, add beer and breadcrumbs to the meat mixture before grilling to achieve both a caramelized flavour and a tasty coating for the meat.

CONDIMENTS

There is no end to the range of condiments that can be made with beer, or if there is I have yet to find it. The trick, of course, is to use beers that specifically enhance the taste of the vinaigrette, jam, mustard or relish being made, rather than merely providing a bit of colour and moisture.

Salad dressings are likely the easiest condiments to enhance with beer, particularly when the beer at hand is a traditional lambic or mixed fermentation beer. Because such brews are by nature acidic, they may be employed in place of whatever vinegar you might otherwise be inclined to use, a framboise ably substituting for a raspberry vinegar, for instance, or a Flemish style red ale taking the place of a balsamic vinegar.

Mustard is one of the craft beer world's biggest complementary product lines, likely rivalling only beer soap as the number one non-clothing brewery spin-off item. You can make yours from mustard seeds, dry mustard powder, and seasonings, all reconstituted by beer – stouts are great and mustard is one condiment that takes on the flavours of hoppy beers quite well – or take a short cut by blending commercial mustards with beer and other ingredients to make a more sauce-like mustard.

Also taking quite kindly to a beer addition are jams and relishes, but here you will be wise in most instances to avoid hoppy beers. Fruit beers will obviously work well in fruity jams, one instance where the bolder the fruit flavour the better, and I enjoy making a caramelised onion relish with the maltiest beer I have in the house, usually juiced up a bit by the addition of a little traditional lambic or, failing that, a dash of vinegar.

USING BEER INGREDIENTS

CONSIDER THIS THE ADVANCED SECTION OF BEER CUISINE, ONE THAT BEGINS WITH A TRIP NOT TO THE GROCERY STORE, BUT YOUR LOCAL HOMEBREW SHOP OR LOCAL BREWERY. BECAUSE WHAT HOPS AND BARLEY MALT CAN DO FOR BEER, THEY CAN ALSO DO FOR FOOD – MINUS THE ALCOHOL, OF COURSE.

IT IS SAID THAT BEER IS LIQUID BREAD, AND SO IT SHOULDN'T SURPRISE YOU THAT ONE OF THE PRIME USES FOR BARLEY MALT IS IN THE BAKING OF BREAD. THE TRICK, HOWEVER, IS THAT THE GRAIN USED SHOULD BE FIRST SPENT, AS IN HAVING BEEN ALREADY EMPLOYED IN THE BREWERY. IF YOUR LOCAL BREWERY IS WILLING TO GIVE UP A CUP OR TWO OF SWEET USED MALT, OR YOU HAVE A BUNCH OF MALT LEFT OVER FROM YOUR LAST HOMEBREW, IT CAN BE COMBINED WITH FLOUR IN ANY NUMBER OF WAYS TO MAKE DELICIOUS BREAD, TRAY BAKES OR COOKIES.

HOPS, ON THE OTHER HAND, ARE BEST USED AS AN AROMATISING AGENT, RATHER THAN A DIRECT INGREDIENT. TO MAKE A FRAGRANT BURGER, FOR EXAMPLE, SIMPLY PLACE THE GROUND MEAT ALONG WITH A HANDFUL OF HOPS IN A SEALED BAG IN THE REFRIGERATOR FOR 24 HOURS OR SO, REMOVE THE HOP PELLETS PRIOR TO MAKING THE BURGERS AND PROCEED WITH YOUR PATTIES AS USUAL. WHILE THE FLAVOUR OF THE BURGER WILL BE LITTLE CHANGED, THE PERCEPTION OF THAT FLAVOUR WILL BECOME MORE FLORAL OR CITRUSSY, DEPENDING ON THE VARIETY OF HOPS USED DUE TO THE INEVITABLE, AND SOMETIMES PROFOUND, INFLUENCE SMELL HAS ON TASTE.

OPPOSITE ABOVE A dash of herbed beer or pale ale can liven up any hollandaise sauce.

OPPOSITE BELOW Mustard seeds or dry mustard powder reconstituted by porter or stout make great beer mustard and work well paired with a pork pie.

BRAISING

Braising is a cooking technique that has all sorts of positives to recommend it. It works best with cheaper, fattier cuts of meat; it requires little in terms of preparation and next to no monitoring; it produces almost invariably moist and tender results; and it's a great use for beer.

I was introduced to the glories of braising with beer many years ago, when Leslie Dillon of the Pyramid Alehouse in Seattle, Washington, contributed a porter-braised lamb shanks recipe to my *Brewpub Cookbook*, reproduced here on page 185. From the moment I finished kitchen testing it, I was hooked.

THE BEAUTY OF BRAISING WITH BEER IS THAT IT PRESENTS A FULL PALETTE OF FLAVOUR OPPORTUNITIES, FROM HOPPY DARK BEERS TO MALTY LIGHT-HUED BEERS AND EVEN ACIDIC LAMBICS OR MIXED FERMENTATION ALES, ALL DEPENDING ON WHAT'S BEING BRAISED AND WHICH OTHER INGREDIENTS MAY BE INVOLVED.

Just choose a beer that you might drink alongside the finished dish to use as your braising liquid, in combination with stock or water or just by itself, and the rest practically takes care of itself.

What's more, once the braising is done, the liquid that remains can form the basis of a delicious, hearty soup. Just throw in a handful of rice or pearl barley and simmer it for an extra hour or so to make lunch for the next day.

DEEP-FRYING

In his *Canadian Craft Beer Cookbook*, food and beer writer David Ort opines that he 'hope(s) we can agree to put two misconceptions about deep frying behind us, namely, that it is difficult and dangerous to do at home'. It is a sentiment I would like to agree with, but I'm not sure that we're quite there yet.

In truth, deep frying truly is quite safe and simple, so long as one follows David's common-sense suggestions of keeping a lid nearby, never overloading the pot and being smart enough not to walk away from a pot of hot oil. And while we're at it, I would add to make sure that you're cooking something delicious!

Deep frying has more than just a safety image problem. It also suffers from its status as the go-to way for preparing food that is meant to be enjoyed with beer. Walk into any pub or sports bar, almost any casual dining restaurant, in fact, and you will see what I mean: oil-soaked onion rings that sported freezer burn an hour earlier; soggy fish and chips with a 2:1 ratio of batter to fish weight; and various known and unknown chicken parts plunged into oil only to reappear minutes later dry, desiccated and yet somehow still greasy. It really is enough to put you off deep frying anything at all.

Fortunately, this need not be the fate of what you fry at home, so long as you don't allow your oil to get old, keep your frying temperature high, and use a top-notch batter.

Beer can help with that last point, since it will not only add lightness and airiness to the fried food thanks to its carbonation, but will also provide greater delicacy by strengthening the bonds in the flour. Obviously, hoppiness needs to be a concern again here, since no one wants an overly bitter batter, and too dark a beer can be visually off-putting even if the results are delicious. But mind your beer addition – batters are actually one of the few culinary methods in which light-bodied lagers excel, with their low bitterness and normally high rate of carbonation – and your deep-fried dishes should emerge delicately crisp and immensely flavourful.

OPPOSITE Deep-fried dumplings practically beg for a flavourful dipping sauce, perhaps made more interesting by the addition of beer.

ABOVE Leftover braised meats can form the base for a tasty stew, especially when also prepared with beer.

While beer and dessert might seem to be by nature incompatible, one needs only look so far as the many varieties of sweet, malty, caramelly and chocolatey ales and lagers on the market today to realize that they can be most harmonious. The key, as ever, is to choose the right flavour profile for the job and avoid excessive hoppiness.

MOST FLEXIBLE OF ALL ARE CHOCOLATE DESSERTS, WHICH CAN ACCEPT A MULTITUDE OF FLAVOURS FROM THE CITRUSSY HOP OF AMERICAN-STYLE PALE ALES AND IPAS TO THE CHOCOLATEY FLAVOURS OF BROWN ALES, STOUTS AND PORTERS.

Beers with a caramel character, such as dubbels, doppelbocks and some brown and amber ales, will add depth to the flavours of ice creams and puddings and pie fillings, while everything from cakes to brownies to cookies can benefit from the residual sugars found in most higher alcohol, sweetly malty beers.

Finally, don't overlook the strengths of sweet fruit beers when planning your dessert course. Normally shunned as overly sugary or saccharinated by beer aficionados, those exact qualities can make them ideal for use in sabayons and flavoured whipped creams, or for poaching fruits like apples and pears.

BEER & CHOCOLATE

By now most people with a serious interest in beer are well aware that their beverage of choice often partners quite well with chocolate. Grab a piece from your local delicatessen, whether a hand-made truffle or something more mainstream and a form of gastronomic nirvana is sure to follow.

What is perhaps less understood are the family resemblances that make this pairing work. I have Peter Slosberg, originator of the once-famous though now bygone Pete's Wicked Ale, to thank for introducing me to these commonalities. For while I knew that both beer and chocolate contain an element of bitterness – beer from hops, of course, and chocolate from cocoa – not knowing a whole lot about

chocolate's production process and history, it hadn't occurred to me that both are fermented foodstuffs with origins that date back many millennia. Further, as Pete pointed out, the key to each is a delicate balancing of the sweet and the bitter.

Beer and chocolate pairing must involve both beers and chocolates that achieve perfect or near-perfect balance. Which is not to say that the beer cannot be predominantly sweet or bitter in character, but that if it is defined by one side of the equation, it must also have the sufficient support of the other. A particularly hop-filled IPA, for instance, can be magnificent when the bitterness is built upon a backbone of malty sweetness, in the same way that sweet, malt-driven beer needs a bracing dose of hops lest it become cloying and overly sugary.

Turn to the chocolate side of the equation and the story is the same. Bitter, high cocoa content chocolate needs a jolt of sweetness to make it palatable, just as sweet chocolate relies upon the bitterness of cocoa to prevent it from becoming a tawdry sugar assault.

Put these together and you have tremendous leeway in pairing flavours, since you can always rely on balance and bitterness to provide harmonies between food and beverage. A sweet truffle with a lemon filling, for example, can be partnered with a double IPA not only because of the citrussy character of the US-grown hops, but also because below the sweetness of the chocolate lies a cocoa bitterness, which the beer will draw forward, to create flavour harmonies. This direction can be pursued in many ways, from 80 per cent cocoa content chocolate matched with a sweet British-style barley wine to a quality candy bar enjoyed alongside a traditional pale ale, so long as attention is paid to the bitterness content in both beer and chocolate.

The exception to this rule is white chocolate, which does not have a bitter component owing to its lack of cocoa solids. This is not to say that it doesn't pair well with beer – sweet and strong golden ales tend to fare well – only that such pairings should not be formed with bitterness in mind.

OPPOSITE Beer and chocolate pairing is all about creating a balance of sweetness and bitterness between the two components.

PAY HEED TO YOUR GLASSWARE

Let's get this straight right away, the shape of your beer glass does make a difference in the way you taste, smell and experience your beer. It's been studied both scientifically and in practice and proven beyond a shadow of a doubt.

That said, you would need to dig pretty deep to find that, say, a slope-sided glass delivers a totally different IPA flavour than would a stemmed and tulip-shaped glass. Or that a Trappist ale offers one set of aromas when served in its trademark chalice-like glass and a distinct and dissimilar set when offered in a snifter. Both examples may be to a degree true, but in a bar or restaurant setting, or at home sharing a few beers with friends, those nuances are unlikely to appear in force.

Better, then, to pay attention to the aesthetics and cleanliness of your beer glassware, since another thing that has been proved time and again is that appearances affect our perceptions of quality.

Simply, a Trappist ale properly poured into a beautiful chalice is going to make a better impression than one served in a plastic cup, and so will in all likelihood deliver a superior taste perception. Ditto the IPA offered in an elegantly curved pint glass as opposed to the clunky, thick-walled 'shaker' pint glass so common in US bars. And the hefeweizen presented in its statuesque, vase-shaped glass instead of a squat, straight-sided mug.

Cleanliness is obviously of prime importance, as well, since a glass streaked with grease or detergent residue will negatively impact the ability of the beer to form and hold its foam, and in extreme cases might even result in off-flavours. If you can reserve glassware at home strictly for beer and keep them out of the dishwasher – away from detergent entirely, in fact, cleaning them with hot water and a hard-bristled brush – then do so and you will find that you pour better tasting and more attractive ales and lagers.

AND ABOVE ALL, KEEP ALL BEER GLASSWARE OUT OF THE FREEZER, AND REQUEST A ROOM TEMPERATURE GLASS WHEN IMBIBING IN THAT CURIOUS BRAND OF BAR OR RESTAURANT THAT RESERVES SPACE IN THE DEEP FREEZE FOR THEIR BEER GLASSES. SINCE EXTREME COLD SUPRESSES AROMA AND MUTES FLAVOUR, A FROSTED BEER GLASS IS ROBBING YOU OF AT LEAST 10–20 PER CENT OF YOUR BEER-DRINKING PLEASURE.

BELOW While different glasses will present different styles of beer well, even the clumsiest, least aesthetically pleasing pint or mug will prove superior to drinking straight from the bottle.

In practical terms, most people, even if they run a bar or restaurant, keep all their beer at a standard temperature, usually one that is a little too cold for the optimal enjoyment of even a pilsner, hefeweizen or Berliner weisse. A wine fridge or cellar helps, since potent, complex ales like barley wines, old ales and Imperial stouts may be kept there at nearer to their optimal temperature. But how many people have one of those at their disposal?

For the rest of us then, enjoying our beer at prime temperature involves planning ahead and taking the bottle or can out of the fridge far enough in advance of its drinking that it has a chance to warm up a bit, or in some cases, a lot.

The average refrigerator is set at a temperature around 2.5°C (36.5°F). Since the flavour of even lighter, crisper beers such as pilsner, helles, kölsch, hefeweizen and wheat ale will be muted at that temperature, it's a smart move to take your next beer out of the fridge around 10–15 minutes before you want to pour it, allowing the temperature to rise a couple of degrees to around 5°C (41°F), bearing in mind that the beer will continue to warm as you drink it. (If you are a slow drinker, a waiting period may not be required at all.)

Ales such as best bitter, traditional IPA and pale ale, brown ale, porter, stout and mild are better served at what is generally referred to as cellar temperature, between 11° and 13°C (52°F and 55.5°F), so half an hour spent outside the fridge will serve them well, even if it might result in a pouring temperature that is a trifle cold. American interpretations of the same beers, American-style pale ale and IPA, hoppy brown ale and such, can generally be served 1–3°C (33.8–37.4°F) cooler to accommodate their more aggressive hoppiness, as can bock, doppelbock, weizenbock and lower-alcohol styles of Belgian origin, such as saison, lambic and many forms of Belgian-style spiced ale.

Strong and dark ales, from dubbel to Scotch ale to barley wine, are all best served at the upper end of cellar temperature or warmer, between 13°C and 16°C (55.5°F

and 61°F), to allow their full range of flavours to express themselves. So take them out of the refrigerator at least a full hour before drinking.

These times and temperatures are only suggested as guidelines. Beers will obviously warm faster when the outside temperature is hotter in the summer, and because of their relative thinness, cans will warm more quickly than bottles. In the end, personal preference should always be the deciding factor, since what is too warm for some will inevitably be too cold for others.

ABOVE Even mass-market beer will have its flavour muted if stored and served at freezing temperatures.

BEER CUISINE AND RECIPES

THE INTERNATIONALIZATION OF BEER CUISINE

BY MOST RECKONINGS, THE FIRST TRULY INTERNATIONAL BEER STYLE WAS PORTER, PRIOR TO WHICH ALL BEER WAS EFFECTIVELY LOCAL. THERE IS A SYMMETRY THEN, IN THE NOTION THAT THE FIRST TRULY INTERNATIONAL BEER AND FOOD PAIRING MIGHT BE SAID TO HAVE INVOLVED THE BEER THAT FOLLOWED PORTER ON ITS GLOBETROTTING VOYAGE, WHICH WAS INDIA PALE ALE; AND THAT ITS PARTNER WAS A CUISINE HEAVILY INFLUENCED BY ANOTHER IMPORT, THE CHILLI PEPPER.

An essential ingredient in most Indian curries, chilli peppers were brought to India in the 16th century by Portuguese traders, while IPA was of course carried there by the British a few centuries later. That the two pair so well was a fluke of time and place, but almost certainly marked the first occasion on which food and drink from two disparate nations were joined together.

CURRY AND IPA ALSO SERVES AS AN EFFECTIVE ILLUSTRATION OF THE IMPORTANT MAXIM THAT, WHEN A TRANS-BORDER BEER AND FOOD PAIRING INVOLVES A NATION WITHOUT A STRONG BREWING HISTORY, CARE SHOULD BE TAKEN NOT TO AUTOMATICALLY DEFAULT TO THE NATIONAL BEER STYLE.

If you have ever enjoyed fiery curries alongside icy bottles of Kingfisher beer, you'll understand immediately the truth behind this axiom. For while the cold lager might seem like it is combatting the spicy heat, in fact it is only the cold that is anaesthetizing your mouth – something which could be even more effectively accomplished with ice water – while the pallid flavour is doing nothing to harmonize with the taste of the dish. Substitute an IPA and the combination gains both flavour and structure.

The logic behind this is simple: the cuisine did not develop alongside the food, so there is nothing to link the two culturally or gastronomically. Mexican food and Corona? Another bust; better to choose a pilsner or American-style pale ale for tacos and burritos, hoppy brown ale or traditional pale ale for molés and so on. Portuguese food with Sagres? More fitting choices would include a dunkel for churrasco chicken, helles for an

LEFT Oysters and porter is a combination born in London dockside pubs, but is known globally as a fine example of beer and food pairing.

açorda, the wonderful Portuguese seafood and bread soup, and a schwarzbier or hefeweizen for the ubiquitous preparations of salt cod. Other good combinations include Pad Thai with pale ale rather than Chang; French onion soup with best bitter over Kronenbourg 1664 and jamón ibérico with a dry bock instead of Cruzcampo.

ABOVE A tempting Far Eastern stir fry that includes spicy chicken and vegetables is best accompanied by a pilsner or pale ale.

While it is tempting to try to figure out a single style or perhaps two or three that can be recommended for the cuisines of those nations which lack strong brewing traditions, the reality is that such short-cut solutions simply do not exist. The only reliable way to find gastronomic joy is to absorb the lessons of the traditional beer lands and add to them present-day guidelines then learn from your own mistakes and successes.

Such is the challenge of food and beer pairing in the modern world. The good news is that the possibilities are exciting and endless.

JOSH OAKES

BEER ADVENTURER

EVERYWHERE

MANY PEOPLE LIKE TO JOKE THAT THEY ARE WILLING TO TRAVEL ALMOST ANYWHERE FOR A BEER, BUT ONLY A SMALL HANDFUL WILL ACTUALLY BE TRUE TO THEIR WORD. JOSH OAKES, EDITOR OF THE CONSUMER BEER REVIEW SITE RATEBEER.COM, CERTAINLY NUMBERS AMONG THAT HANDFUL, HAVING SPENT THE BETTER PART OF THE LAST SEVERAL YEARS TOURING THE GLOBE IN SEARCH OF NEW EXPERIENCES, EXCITING FOODS AND, OF COURSE, GREAT BEER.

When I first met Josh, he was an avid beer enthusiast, with his feet firmly planted in our mutual hometown of Toronto. A move to Vancouver was the first hint of his nomadic tendencies, but even then it was several years before he hit the road in force. When he finally embraced his wanderlust he did so with unrestrained enthusiasm. Along the way, Josh has experienced an enviable number of opportunities for beer and food pairing, including many that would normally be considered the stuff of foodie fantasies.

'IN MUCH OF THE WORLD, PEOPLE ARE DRINKING EITHER YELLOW FIZZY BEER OR THEY ARE JUST LEARNING ABOUT CRAFT BEER BY CRIBBING FROM THE GERMAN OR AMERICAN TRADITIONS,' JOSH RECOUNTS, 'PAIRINGS IN SUCH PLACES CAN BE PRETTY BASIC, BUT WHEREVER PEOPLE DRINK A LOT OF BEER THEY HAVE FUN THINGS THAT THEY LIKE TO EAT WITH BEER.'

Among the 'fun things' he cites are herring bars in Poland, where basic pilsner is partnered with various preparations of the famously versatile fish, hoppy South African pale ale with piri-piri chicken livers and, in Siberian Russia, what he singles out as the best smoked fish in the world enjoyed with lagers from 'independent breweries – still industrial, but making more characterful beers'.

That last point is something that colours Josh's world view and fuels his optimism. While he is quick to admit that, in much of the world, mass market lagers remain the go-to for the majority of beer drinkers, he believes that the door is wide open for the evolution of beer and food pairing.

'We're just barely scratching the surface, I think', he says, 'One of the best combinations I've had lately was at Bar Volo (in Toronto, Canada), matching their anchovies with Trois Mousquetaires Hors Série Gose, a pairing that would have been all but impossible to find even a couple of years ago, since goses in southern Ontario simply did not exist.' If change of that dramatic nature can happen in so short a time, he muses, 'imagine what can occur in other places in the near future'.

Warming further to his theme, Josh adds that some of his best pairings 'still live inside my daydreams – getting that perfect porter for *molé negro*, finding the best fruity Belgian blonde for *poisson cru*, and things like that. I'm excited for the future'.

That said, Josh also stresses the importance of context in terms of the enjoyment of food and drink, that while the food and the beer are important, so is 'the moment'.

'The worst thing we do is compartmentalize food and drink,' he says, 'You still see restaurants with extensive wine lists that completely mail it in when it comes to beer. You see great beer bars or brewpubs that are stuck in a burger-pizza-nacho vortex. You can do those things well, but too few places are putting it all together. I think that will change'.

OPPOSITE ABOVE Josh Oakes is a habitual traveller and a beer adventurer, seeking out new and exciting craft beers wherever his travels take him.

OPPOSITE BELOW From British and South African pale ales to German lagers and Canadian gose, it is the diversity of flavour and character of world beers that keeps Josh Oakes motivated during his ongoing beer and food journey.

JOON OU
SEASONALITY SPECIALIST

BAIRD BREWING COMPANY, GREATER TOKYO AREA, JAPAN

'JAPANESE CUISINE THRIVES ON SEASONALITY', SAYS JOON OU, THE KOREAN-BORN AND OREGON-RAISED EXECUTIVE CHEF FOR JAPAN'S BAIRD BREWING. 'WHETHER IT BE FRESH VEGETABLES, FISH, OR SPECIFIC DISHES, MOST VENDORS AND RESTAURANTS IN JAPAN RECOGNIZE THE IMPORTANCE OF EATING BY SEASONS. I THINK THE SAME GOES WITH MAKING BEER'.

And so, in a quick three sentences, Joon spells out the philosophy he has devised to manage the menus at Baird's four taprooms, adding that with the brewery's dozen regular brands and 'many more' seasonal styles, his biggest challenge as a chef is developing enough dishes to go with all of the beers.

'TWENTY YEARS AGO, ALL YOU SAW IN JAPAN WERE LAGERS, WHICH ARE GENERALLY WELL MADE AND GO VERY WELL WITH FRESH SUSHI AND LIGHTLY FRIED FOODS,' SAYS JOON, 'BUT AFTER THEIR FIRST TASTE OF A MALTY PORTER OR A HOPPY IPA, THESE JAPANESE BEER LOVERS HAD THEIR EYES OPENED TO A WORLD BEYOND LAGERS. PEOPLE BEGAN TO REALIZE THAT THERE WAS A BEER FIT FOR ANY PALATE, MUCH LIKE THE MANY VARIETIES OF JAPANESE SAKÉ AND SHOCHU.'

That proliferation of lagers was a direct result of the utter dominance of the Japanese Big Four brewers – Sapporo, Kirin, Asahi and Suntory – and their largely Germanic origins. It was a supremacy that was easy for the big brewers to maintain, as well, since the strict brewery licencing laws of the time required any operating brewery to produce a minimum of 20,000 hl (17,000 barrels) of beer per year, an amount inconceivable for a typical craft brewery start-up.

Those regulations were changed in the mid 1990s, however, and breweries burst upon the scene with astonishing speed, at one point exceeding a rate of one brewery per month. With these new breweries came the new beers, at first in the traditional European styles, then under the influence of the US craft brewing scene, and finally more imaginative and Japan-inspired brews.

This diversity is reflected in the Baird Brewing range, which extends from lighter lagers to Imperial IPAs and seasonal beers flavoured with Japanese fruits like yuzu and mikan. So when it comes to partnering beers with his seasonal menus, Joon hardly finds himself hampered.

'I have a large playing field when it comes to pairing our beers with food' he says, 'Anything from delicate raw seafood to roasted meats are fair game.' And in fact, he notes that the general emphasis Japanese cooks place upon the raw ingredients, rather than embellishments such as seasoning and sauces, make pairing perhaps a bit easier than it might be with other cuisines.

'Very traditional Japanese dishes are almost always centered on the flavours of the ingredients themselves with very little tampering and modest seasoning.' says Joon, 'Something on the lighter side like a lager or wit would pair well with more delicate Japanese ingredients like fresh seafood and tofu, (but) the more modern iterations of Japanese food like fried pork cutlets, grilled and skewered meats with sweet, salty sauces, and flour-based savoury pancakes, these types of dishes go very well with any number of hoppy or malty ales'.

OPPOSITE ABOVE AND BELOW Joon Ou of the Baird Brewing Company in Tokyo, Japan specializes in seasonal cuisine and is dedicated to providing suitable beer matches for his dishes.

JAPANESE BEER FRIED CHICKEN (KARA-AGE)

JOON OU, THE EXECUTIVE CHEF AT JAPAN'S BAIRD BREWING, NOTES THAT THIS JAPANESE FRIED CHICKEN DISH IS CHINESE INFLUENCED, ALTHOUGH THE USE OF LAGER DOES MAKE IT A LITTLE UNUSUAL.

SERVES 4 OR 5 AS A SNACK OR STARTER

5 chicken breasts, boneless and skinless
1 tbsp salt
2 tbsp white sugar
pinch black pepper

2 large cloves garlic, finely minced
1 thumb-sized piece of ginger, peeled and finely minced

1 tbsp soy sauce
240ml (8fl oz) Vienna lager (Joon uses Baird's Numazu Lager)

Potato Starch (Katakuriko, available at Asian food shops) or corn starch
Vegetable oil for frying

METHOD

1   Cut each chicken breast into 1- or 2-inch pieces.
2   In a bowl large enough to hold the chicken and all the liquids, mix together all the other ingredients except for the potato starch. Add the chicken pieces and make sure they are fully submerged. Cover with a lid or plastic wrap and marinate chicken in the refrigerator for at least 4 hours.
3   In a large pot, heat between 2.5cm and 5cm (1-2in) of oil until it reaches roughly 180ºC/350ºF. Remove the chicken pieces from the marinade and allow any excess to drain off. Dredge each piece in potato starch and fry until golden brown.
4   Serve with shredded cabbage and mayonnaise for dipping.

RECOMMENDED BEER

Pair with a sturdy Czech-style pilsner or a British-style pale ale.

STOUT-STEAMED EDAMAME

BAIRD BREWING EXECUTIVE CHEF JOON OU'S TWIST ON THIS TRADITIONAL JAPANESE SNACK COATS THE BRIGHT GREEN PODS WITH A LIGHTLY BITTER AND MALTY STOUT SYRUP.

SERVES 4 OR 5 AS A SNACK OR STARTER

1 kg (2.2lbs) frozen edamame (in the pod)

1–2 bottles dry stout (Joon uses Baird Brewing's Shimaguni Stout)

Sea salt, generous pinch
Freshly ground black pepper, generous pinch

Ground chilli flakes or Shichimi spice (found in Asian food stores, optional)

METHOD

1 In a large pot on a medium-high heat, add the frozen edamame and enough beer to cover half of the beans. Heat until boiling, then reduce to medium heat and continue cooking the beans, stirring from time to time to keep them from burning.

2 When the beer has turned into a thin syrup, turn off the heat and toss the beans with the seasonings. Serve warm.

RECOMMENDED BEER

A pleasant counterpoint to the sticky stout syrup would be a fresh German helles lager.

DANIEL GOH

CRAFT BEER EVANGELIST

THE GOOD BEER COMPANY, SINGAPORE

GOH OPENED THE GOOD BEER COMPANY IN 2011, DETERMINED TO INJECT A VARIETY OF QUALITY BEERS INTO SINGAPORE'S VIBRANT FOOD, BUT RATHER STAID BEER CULTURE. A FEW YEARS LATER, IN JANUARY 2014, HE JOINED FORCES WITH HIS ERSTWHILE COMPETITOR, KWOK MENG-CHAO, OWNER OF THE WEST-CENTRAL BREWERS' CRAFT BOTTLE SHOP, TO OPEN SMITH STREET TAPS, A DRAUGHT-ONLY STALL MERE PACES AWAY FROM GOH'S GOOD BEER ORIGINAL.

Wander around the second floor of Singapore's sprawling Chinatown Complex on Smith Street for long enough and, wedged between 'hawker stalls' selling all manner of Singaporean street foods, you will eventually come upon the Good Beer Company. Arrive at the right time and you will also find the smiling face of Daniel Goh.

With two locations housed among nearly 200 food purveyors, Daniel has had ample opportunity to not only learn everything there is to know about Singapore's young craft beer market, but also help steer the course of food and beer pairing in the city-state.

'MUCH OF SINGAPORE'S CULTURE IS CENTRED AROUND FOOD, AND SINGAPOREANS HAVE ALWAYS BEEN VERY OPEN AND EXCITED ABOUT DIFFERENT FLAVOURS OF CUISINES FROM AROUND THE WORLD,' HE EXPLAINS, 'IT'S THE SAME WITH BEER – AS PALATES OPEN UP TO THE POSSIBILITIES WITH DIFFERENT BEER STYLES AND TASTES, WE'RE DEFINITELY EXPLORING HOW BEERS CAN PAIR WITH FOOD.'

And the possibilities are myriad. While Daniel describes Singapore's street food culture as the result of an exciting mix of its Chinese, Indian and Malay cultures, he is quick to add that culinary influences from other parts of the world are also at work. The result, he says, is a 'near infinite' number of potential pairings involving the 60 or more bottled beers and 10 draught beers stocked at the two stalls.

'We often get people coming to us, showing us their food and asking what beers would pair well with them', he says,

'We've even had some food sellers come to us asking us to recommend their food to customers based on what beers we carry!'

For the uninitiated, Daniel offers that Singapore street food standards tend to be rather generously seasoned and often quite spicy, citing in particular what he says might be the most famous Singapore original, chilli crab, which sees the crustacean stir-fried in a sweet and sour chilli sauce. Such foods, he says, are tricky to pair successfully with robustly flavoured beers.

'The styles that do work are pale ales, whose bitterness helps cut through the fat and oiliness inherent in many local dishes,' he says, 'And saisons and white ales (Belgian-style wheat beers) also work brilliantly, with their bright effervescence and fruitiness refreshing the palate and helping calm down and yet complement the spiciness of our food'.

When speaking of the future of Singaporean craft beer in general and beer and food pairing in particular, Daniel is nothing if not enthusiastically optimistic, seeing opportunity in many beer styles not yet popular or even entirely understood by the locals.

'We still need to consider what kind of beers and flavours customers like, as well as what beers work with their food,' he says, observing that this can hamper this suggested pairing, 'For example, a Belgian Flemish red ale may work very well with bak chor mee – a noodle dish laced with chilli and vinegar – but it's a style that's just not very popular with locals yet'.

OPPOSITE Daniel Goh is often to be seen smiling behind the beer pumps at Smith Street Taps, sister stall to his Good Beer Company, in Singapore's Chinatown district.

JESSE VALLINS
THE VOICE OF RESTRAINT

**THE SAINT TAVERN,
TORONTO, CANADA**

SINCE WELL BEFORE I HELPED OPEN THE TORONTO RESTAURANT AND BAR, BEERBISTRO, I HAD THROUGH BEER EVENTS AND TASTINGS BECOME ACQUAINTED WITH A YOUNG COOK AND BEER ENTHUSIAST BY THE NAME OF JESSE VALLINS. SO IT WAS NO SURPRISE WHEN, EVEN BEFORE WE WENT PUBLIC WITH OUR PLANS TO CREATE THE CITY'S FIRST BEER CUISINE RESTAURANT, BEFORE WE EVEN HAD A LOCATION SECURED, IN FACT, I WAS GETTING EMAILS FROM JESSE PETITIONING FOR A POSITION IN THE KITCHEN.

'I WAS A BEER GEEK FROM PRETTY MUCH THE MOMENT I BECAME OF LEGAL DRINKING AGE,' HE RECALLS, 'SO WITH MY INTEREST IN COOKING, IT WAS ONLY NATURAL THAT I WOULD GRAVITATE TOWARDS MAKING DISHES WITH BEER'.

Given such enthusiasm, it didn't take much else to convince principle owner and executive chef Brian Morin to give this young man a shot, and despite his relative youth, it was equally not long before Jesse was working his way through the ranks to the position of sous chef. Many were the beer dinners he and I orchestrated alongside Brian and other key members of the staff, and many were the beers we shared afterwards while dissecting the pairings and debating areas for possible improvement next time.

Eventually, however, Jesse's creativity and ambition took him to the helm of his own kitchen, first in a restaurant down the road called Trevor and ultimately to the crosstown tavern-restaurant, The Saint. Along the way, he cemented his reputation as Toronto's 'Sausage King' by winning the annual inter-restaurant Sausage League three years in a row, so it is perhaps not surprising that when he talks today about beer cuisine, the use of beer as the liquid for sausages is one of the first topics raised.

'People forget that you need to mind your fat ratios and your moisture when making sausage,' he says, "I like about 75 ml (2 ½fl oz) of liquid per kilo of meat, and you need to work it in well, since failing to do so will affect the texture of the sausage'.

That said, Jesse is perhaps surprisingly reticent about suggesting beer as the default liquid for all sausages.

'An IPA works well with spicy food, so it works also well in a spicy sausage', he notes, 'But my philosophy is that beer really needs to be the number one liquid of choice in any recipe, not just something that you use because you want to say there is beer in a dish. If you use it for any other reason, it takes away from the dish and makes it gimmicky.'

For this reason Jesse says that he has, over the years, become more of a proponent of pairing food with beer than he is of cooking with it, although he still does a fair amount of the latter at the Saint, principally in creating the beer-poached prunes, mustards and various other condiments he offers with the restaurant's steaks and sausages.

'I've always thought of eating in a restaurant as an experience, and making a great pairing, whether it's with beer or wine or a cocktail, adds to that experience in a way that forcing beer into a dish never could,' he notes, 'For that reason, I'd rather create a great pairing than I would cook a dish with a great beer.'

OPPOSITE ABOVE Starting his career at beerbistro in Toronto, Canada, Jessie Vallins has gone on to become chef at tavern-restaurant The Saint in the same city.

OPPOSITE BELOW Jessie Vallins makes his own delicious beer mustard (see page 137 for recipe).

STOUT BROWN SAUCE

ALTHOUGH HE PLIES HIS TRADE IN CANADA, THERE IS A LOT OF ENGLISH INFLUENCE IN THE COOKING OF JESSE VALLINS, SO IT'S UNSURPRISING THAT HE DEVELOPED THIS TASTY BROWN SAUCE FOR SERVING WITH STEAK AT THE SAINT.

160g (5½oz) dates, pitted
160g (5½oz) raisins
60ml (2fl oz) + 1 tbsp Worcestershire sauce

2 tsp molasses
235ml (8fl oz) stout
30g (1oz) tamarind pulp
295ml (10fl oz) malt vinegar

60ml (2fl oz) + 1 tbsp orange juice, freshly squeezed
50g (2 oz) Dijon mustard
4 tsp kosher salt

Half a Spanish onion, diced
3 cloves garlic, crushed
Pinch of curry powder

METHOD

1 In a saucepan over medium heat, combine all the ingredients and cook until soft, stirring occasionally. Transfer to a blender or food processor and blend until smooth. Store refrigerated for up to 2 weeks.

BEER MUSTARD

IF YOU'RE THE LOCAL 'SAUSAGE KING,' THEN YOU'D BETTER HAVE A PRETTY GOOD MUSTARD RECIPE OR TWO TO GO ALONG WITH YOUR LINKS. THIS ONE FROM JESSE VALLINS AT THE SAINT FITS THE BILL.

3 tbsp yellow mustard seeds

3 tbsp brown mustard seeds

1½ tbsp dry mustard powder

4 tbsp malt vinegar

170ml (6fl oz) dark beer, a porter, stout or dubbel

2 tbsp barley malt extract*

1½ tsp sea salt

* Barley malt extract is a thick, molasses-like liquid used in baking. It can be found in bulk and in baking supply stores.

METHOD

1 In a non-reactive container, combine the mustard seeds, beer and vinegar. Cover and leave overnight.

2 The next day, place the mixture in a food processor and pulse until a coarse paste is formed. Transfer to a *bain marie* over medium heat, or a metal bowl suspended over a pot of simmering water, and add the remaining ingredients. Stir constantly for approximately 20 minutes until the mustard thickens. Transfer to a jar and store refrigerated for up to one month.

SEAN PAXTON

ITINERANT HOMEBREW CHEF

SONOMA, CALIFORNIA, USA

NORTHERN CALIFORNIA RESIDENT SEAN PAXTON IS LIKELY THE MOST PROMINENT, AND ALMOST CERTAINLY THE MOST ADEPT, PROPONENT OF ALL FACETS OF BEER CUISINE IN THE UNITED STATES TODAY. A PROFESSIONAL CHEF AND CULINARY EDUCATOR WHO OPERATES UNDER THE BANNER OF 'THE HOMEBREW CHEF', SEAN DISCOVERED THE JOYS OF COOKING WITH BEER SHORTLY AFTER HE BEGAN BREWING AT HOME AND HAS NOT LOOKED BACK SINCE.

'Almost 20 years ago, I started homebrewing', he says, 'And after my second batch, I realized that I had a lot of extra beer. I was cooking and needed some liquid, and didn't have any wine, so I used the beer'.

That dish, the very first in which the young chef discovered the utility of beer in cooking, is one he still prepares today. 'I caramelized shallots with butter and added some thyme and morel mushrooms to the pan. Then I deglazed the whole thing with doppelbock, added a bit of veal stock, and served it over a veal chop. The combination created a really savoury character, with a lot of umami qualities'.

In the years since, Sean has honed his craft principally through private consultations and bespoke beer dinners, often creating epic, long-remembered occasions in the process.

'I'VE HAD RESTAURANTS BEFORE, AND IF I DID HAVE ONE TODAY, I KNOW THAT I'D BE STUCK AT THAT ONE RESTAURANT,' HE SAYS OF HIS CHEF-FOR-HIRE STATUS, 'BY BEING INDEPENDENT I'M ABLE TO GET OUT AND TRAVEL (WHICH) BRINGS ME A BROADER PERSPECTIVE ON FOOD AND BEER.'

Broader, indeed. In the US craft beer world, Sean's prowess in beer cuisine is legendary. His use of beer and beer ingredients in cooking is nothing less than inspired and extends to such complicated procedures as raising a pig on spent grain, ageing the meat in hop sacks stuffed with pelletized hops and finally roasting the pig over dried hop vines. To him, the end result is always worth the effort, no matter how involved that effort might be.

'When you drink a beer and enjoy it, that's one thing', he says, 'But it's exploiting the flavours in the beer, contrasting and complementing, adding those different flavours in different ways, that's what makes cooking with beer such a blast'.

It's a passion he relishes in sharing with others, especially since he views beer and beer cuisine as being glaring omissions in the education of most chefs. Having known Sean for many years, I can vouch for this latter belief, since it is a topic we almost inevitably revisit over beers whenever our travels bring us to the same place at the same time.

'Cooking schools don't even teach their students about bitterness,' Sean insists, 'wine has no bitterness to speak of, so that element gets lost, and many beers have astringency, too, which a lot of cooks just don't know how to deal with. I see them taking a roasty, astringent stout and reducing it, making that astringency harsh, and I wonder "why are you doing this?" It's because they just don't know'.

So long as the Homebrew Chef continues his evangelical ways, it's a knowledge gap that appears destined to shrink, one professional chef or amateur cook at a time.

OPPOSITE Sean Paxton is known as 'The Homebrew Chef', having started his adventures in cooking with beer more than 20 years ago.

OVERLEAF ABOVE Trainee chefs enjoy learning from Sean's high level of beer and food knowledge.

OVERLEAF BELOW Oxtail and pearl barley soup is a simple and hearty dish made more delicious by the addition of dark ale to the stock.

OXTAIL AND PEARL BARLEY SOUP

ALTHOUGH HIS CREATIONS CAN RUN TO EXTREMES – THINK AROMATIZING AN ENTIRE SUCKLING PIG WITH HOPS – CALIFORNIA CHEF SEAN PAXTON ALSO APPRECIATES SIMPLE AND HEARTY DISHES, LIKE THIS WONDERFULLY FILLING SOUP THAT HE SAYS IS 'ONE OF THOSE SOUPS THAT ALMOST EVERYONE CAN MAKE'.

SERVES 6

2 tbsp olive oil

1 oxtail, 900g–1.3kg (2–3lb) weight, cut between each vertebra

salt and pepper to taste

2 large onions, peeled and chopped

1 leek, washed, cleaned and sliced

4 shallots, peeled and chopped

8–10 garlic cloves, peeled and sliced

4 carrots, peeled and sliced

450g (1lb) mushrooms, crimini, cleaned and quartered

2 tbsp fresh thyme leaves

4 bay leaves

1 × 400g (14oz) can chopped tomatoes

1l (36fl oz) dark ale, choose from brown ale, smoked porter, stout or similar

1l (36fl oz) beef or chicken stock, preferably homemade

225g (8oz) pearl barley

Half bunch flat leaf parsley, chopped

Smoked salt and black pepper to taste

METHOD

1   Heat the oil in a large pot on medium-high heat. Season oxtail with salt and pepper on all sides and brown in the oil. Remove and set aside.

2   Add onions and sauté for 4–5 minutes. Add all other vegetables and cook for 8-10 minutes, until they start to brown. Remove half the vegetables from the pot and add herbs and tomatoes. Cook until heated through.

3   Return the oxtail to the pot and deglaze with 700ml (24 fl oz) of the beer. Add the stock and bring to a boil. Reduce heat to low, cover and simmer for one hour.

4   Add the pearl barley, stir and simmer for a further hour.

5   After 2 hours, add the reserved sautéed vegetables and remaining beer to the soup. Simmer for 30 minutes. Remove oxtail and strip meat from the bones. Lightly chop the meat and return to pot. Remove bay leaves and check seasoning. Add some water if too thick and season. Add the chopped parsley, stir and serve.

RECOMMENDED BEER

Some people will tell you that soup, being a liquid itself, doesn't need a beverage pairing. Those people have never enjoyed this soup with a glass of cellar temperature smoked porter.

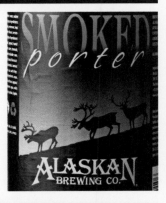

BEER BRAISED PORK BELLY WITH A CREOLE SEASONING

WHAT BEER CHEF DOESN'T LIKE PORK BELLY, AKA UNCURED BACON? CERTAINLY NOT SEAN PAXTON, WHO NOTES THAT THIS DISH CAN BE SERVED AS A STAND-ALONE MAIN COURSE OR PORTIONED OUT MORE MODESTLY AS A PROTEIN IN A MULTI-COURSE MENU.

MAKES 18 × 100G (4OZ) PORTIONS

1l (36 fl oz) bitter or mild ale (not hoppy, Sean uses Firestone Walker DBA)

1 tbsp brown sugar
1 tbsp sea salt
2 tsp thyme, fresh

2 bay leaves
1–4 tbsp Cajun Spice Blend, depending on heat level

2.2kg (5 lb) pork belly, skin removed

METHOD

BEER BRAISED PORK BELLY DIRECTIONS

1   Pre-heat oven to 130°C/250°F/ gas mark ½. In a pan just large enough to hold the belly – 22 × 33 cm (9 × 13in) should work – combine all the ingredients except the belly and mix well.

2   Add the pork belly, cover with aluminum foil and place in the centre of the oven and braise for 4–6 hours, until it is tender but not falling apart.

3   Once cooked, allow the pork belly to cool in the braising liquid. To flatten it out and make it easier to manage, cover the pork and liquid with cling film and place a smaller flat pan on top, weighing it down with canned food. Leave in refrigerator overnight.

4   The next day, remove the pork from the braising liquid and cut into pieces, 2.5cm (1in) square for a starter or 5 × 7.5cm (2 × 3in) for a main course.

BLACKENED PORK BELLY DIRECTIONS

5   Heat a cast-iron frying pan on a high heat. Sprinkle the pork with Cajun spice and press down.

6   Add a few tablespoons of butter to the pan, let it melt and, using tongs, place the pork belly seasoned side down. Cook for 1-2 minutes, searing and blackening the spices. Use your extractor fan as the meat will smoke.

7   Turn each of the pieces over and let them warm through. Remove from the pan and serve immediately.

RECOMMENDED BEER

Which beer you choose for this will obviously depend on how spicy you make it, but for a mellow heat try a dunkel or best bitter. For something more spicy, try a hoppy hefeweizen or hopfenweisse.

LUCY SAUNDERS

AUTHOR, 'BEERCOOK' AND BEER CUISINE EXPLORER

MILWAUKEE, WISCONSIN, USA

LUCY SAUNDERS SAYS THAT SHE STARTED COOKING WHEN SHE WAS SEVEN YEARS OLD. SHE'S LESS SPECIFIC ABOUT WHEN SHE FIRST TRIED BEER, BUT NOTES THAT SHE HAS 'ALWAYS LOVED' ITS TASTE, SO IT WAS PERHAPS PREDESTINED THAT SHE SHOULD ONE DAY PUT THE TWO TOGETHER.

That day arrived during her studies in English literature, when as part of an independent studies project Saunders decided to reconstruct a Medieval English feast. 'In recreating the recipes,' she says, 'I discovered that cooking with beer was a big part of life back then, largely because the water supply was so unsafe'.

Even though she graduated into a job in copy editing rather than one in the kitchen, Lucy's fascination with beer and food continued through collecting recipes that involved beer and, eventually, beginning to experiment with dishes of her own. Along the way, she got into writing and ghosted a couple of cookbooks, as well as authoring one of her own. Her status as 'The Beercook' was sealed, however, with the publication of *Cooking with Beer* in 1996, one of a small handful of early American beer cuisine cookbooks.

Sharing an interest in cooking and pairing food with beer, as well as authoring competing books – my own *Brewpub Cookbook* came out a year after Lucy's book – could have positioned us as adversaries, but instead it made us friends. Since *Cooking with Beer*, Lucy has published three more cookbooks involving beer, most recently, *Dinner in the Beer Garden,* an almost all-vegetarian book that stems in part from her fascination with the growing number of brewery restaurants that feature kitchen gardens. Along the way I have remained among her greatest fans.

Although she works full-time writing recipes and teaching beer cuisine basics, Lucy is not one of those absolutists who will insist that a specific beer is the only possible one to either use in or pair with a given recipe.

'PEOPLE'S TASTE BUDS ARE THEIR OWN,' SHE SAYS, 'EVERYONE HAS DIFFERENT LEVELS OF SENSITIVITY TO DIFFERENT FLAVOURS, SO I ENCOURAGE PEOPLE TO USE THE KIND OF BEERS THEY ENJOY EVEN IF – GASP! – THAT MEANS USING A STYLE OF BEER NOT SUGGESTED FOR THE RECIPE.'

Obviously, there are limits to how far this approach can go, since the substitution of, say, a highly bitter IPA for a sweet and malty strong dark or Scotch ale is unlikely to produce an equivalent result. But even so, Lucy is undaunted, noting that the current crop of young chefs is the first in the United States to grow up during a time that craft beer was simply part of the landscape, rather than being exotic and unusual. As such, she says, we're going to see a lot of exciting and unconventional beer cuisine dishes appearing over the course of the next ten years or so.

For those non-professional chefs seeking to join the party, Lucy offers some advice for adapting your favourite recipes to beer cuisine recipes. 'Test the recipe carefully and don't make a straight one-to-one substitution of beer for the liquid,' she cautions, 'The beer will have different properties, such as residual sugars and such, which can change the taste or the process that needs to be followed for a recipe. Chicken marinated in a very sweet dark ale, for example, will caramelize and char on the grill quickly because of those sugars'.

Sage advice from someone now in her third decade of beer cuisine experimentation.

OPPOSITE Lucy Saunders wrote one of the first and best beer cuisine cookbooks, *Cooking with Beer* in 1996. She has gone on to write several more.

HOP-AGED CHEDDAR AND TOMATO GRILLED CHEESE SANDWICH

THIS RECIPE FROM LUCY SAUNDERS, WHO NOT SURPRISINGLY CALLS THE U.S. 'CHEESE STATE' OF WISCONSIN HOME, USES AN INFUSION TECHNIQUE TO GIVE CHEDDAR CHEESE A GENTLE HOP FLAVOUR. ALTHOUGH IT MIGHT SEEM UNCONVENTIONAL, IT IS REALLY JUST AN ADAPTATION OF AN AGE-OLD CHEESEMAKING TECHNIQUE CALLED *AFFINAGE* (AGEING CHEESE).

MAKES 2 SANDWICHES

For the cheese
25–50g (1–2oz) dried hops in flower or pelletized form (available from homebrew shops or a friendly local brewer)

150g (6oz) block of Cheddar cheese

For the sandwich
3 tbsp butter, softened
4 slices wholegrain bread

100–150g (4–6oz) hop-aged Cheddar, grated or thinly sliced
1 heirloom tomato, about 285g (10oz), sliced thick (2 tomatoes, if small)

4–5 fresh basil leaves, shredded
2 tbsp brown seed or coarse ground mustard

METHOD

1   At least one day in advance, place the hops in the bottom of a glass or stainless steel container. Top with a square of parchment paper to keep the hops from having direct contact with the cheese, and then place the cheese on top. Seal and let infuse in the refrigerator overnight. Taste the next day to see if the cheese is 'hoppy' enough; age further if not.

2   To make the sandwich heat a heavy saucepan or griddle (cast iron is best) over medium heat. Butter the bread slices on one side.

3   Place two slices of bread, buttered side down, on the hot pan or griddle. Arrange half of the grated cheese over the bread and top with tomato slices. Sprinkle with the shredded basil.

4   Place the remaining Cheddar over the tomatoes. Spread mustard on unbuttered side of the bread. Top the tomatoes with bread slices, buttered side up. Top with a lid or tent with foil, and cook several more minutes.

5   Check that bread is golden brown and cheese is melting.

Flip and continue to cook uncovered until other side is toasted, another 2–3 minutes. Serve with salad.

RECOMMENDED BEER

Pair this with a dryly hoppy pale ale or best bitter, if possible one hopped with the same variety used to infuse the cheese.

EDUARDO PASSERELLI

BRAZILIAN BEER & FOOD EXPLORER

SÃO PAULO, BRAZIL

THE FIRST TIME I VISITED BRAZIL, I WAS INVITED TO THE ANNIVERSARY PARTY OF A BAR IN SÃO PAULO NAMED MELOGRANO. BY THIS POINT, I HAD ALREADY BEEN AMAZED BY THE YOUNG BUT INCREDIBLY ENTHUSIASTIC CRAFT BEER MOVEMENT IN SOUTH AMERICA'S LARGEST COUNTRY AND ASTOUNDED BY THE LANDMARK GOOD BEER BAR, FRANGÓ, WHICH REMAINS A FAVOURITE TODAY. WHAT I FOUND AT MELOGRANO COMPLETED MY TRIO OF SURPRISES.

Here was a place that not only specialized in presenting Brazilian craft brews, and had its own very impressive ale brewed by a local operation, to boot, but also placed great emphasis on the pairing of those beers with the various dishes on its menu. To place this in context, Brazil's craft beer scene was only a few years old at the time, whereas it took the restaurants of the United States and Canada decades to recognize the merits of beer and food pairing.

The author of this piece of gastronomic foresight was a young man named Eduardo Passerelli, Edu, for short. The moment I met him I somehow knew that I would be hearing much more from and about him in the future.

Most great beer enthusiasts have a story about their epiphany moment, and Edu's involved a German hefeweizen when he was 19 years old. Already in the restaurant business at the time, the beer stimulated in him an interest to find out much, much more about not just beer, but all aspects of food and drink, a curiosity that eventually led him to chef school.

It was there, during a wine and food pairing seminar, that Edu first began to think about partnering food with beer, and not long thereafter started his blog, Edu Recomenda, or Edu Recommends. Two years later, he became the owner and manager of Melograno and, for perhaps the first time ever, brought the marriage of beer and food to a Brazilian restaurant.

At Edu's current restaurant, Aconchego Carioca in São Paulo, beer and food matching is less on the menu than it was at Melograno, but the guidance is still there for those who desire it.

'Aconchego is a typical Brazilian "boteco" where you can find simple, but very good food in a casual atmosphere', he explains, 'So while our waiters know the food and beer pairings, they will only suggest it when the customer asks.'

And some of those pairings?

'OUR MOST FAMOUS DISH IS FEIJOADA – A SORT OF MEAT AND BEAN STEW TYPICAL OF BRAZIL – AND IT WORKS WELL WITH SCHWARZBIER, RAUCHBIER AND EVEN A WITBIER FOR CONTRAST', EDU SAYS, 'OR BOBÓ DE CAMARÃO, MADE WITH SHRIMPS, MANIOC AND COCONUT MILK, WHICH IS PERFECT WITH AN IPA! AND FOR DESSERT WE MAKE A DISH FROM TAPIOCA, COCONUT MILK, MOLASSES AND CACHAÇA SAUCE THAT IS INCREDIBLE WITH 3 LOBOS BRAVO, A STRONG PORTER AGED IN AMBURANA WOOD FROM THE AMAZON.'

Proof that the partnership of good beer and food can transcend not only national borders and styles of cuisine, but even deeply rooted culinary traditions.

OPPOSITE Eduardo Passerelli has been a pioneer of beer and food pairing in Brazil, where he has his own restaurant, Aconchego Carioca in São Paulo.

PORK RIBS WITH BEER AND CHOCOLATE

THE COMBINATION OF CHOCOLATE WITH THE DARK MALTS OF THE BEER ARE KEY TO THE RICH FLAVOURS IN THIS DISH CREATED BY EDU PASSARELLI AT ACONCHEGO CARIOCA. SINCE THE BEER WILL REDUCE QUITE A BIT DURING COOKING, BE SURE TO USE ONE THAT IS VERY LOW IN HOPPINESS.

SERVES 4–6

1kg (2.2lbs) pork ribs
350g (12oz) onion, diced
Salt, white pepper to taste

600ml (20fl oz) dunkel, brown ale, Scotch ale or strong dark ale

2 tbsp butter
1 tbsp brown sugar

50g (2oz) bittersweet chocolate

METHOD

1 A minimum of 12 hours in advance, combine the onion, salt and pepper and half the beer in a sealable container, then add the ribs. Seal and leave to refrigerate for at least 12 hours, shaking occasionally to recoat the ribs with the marinade.

2 When ready to cook, preheat oven to 180°C/350°F/gas mark 4. Remove ribs from the marinade and place on a greased baking sheet. Place in oven to start cooking.

3 To make the basting sauce using a sieve, separate the onion and the marinade, being careful to reserve the liquid. In a deep saucepan on medium heat, sauté the onion until very soft, gradually adding the marinade and remaining beer bit by bit as you do. When the onion is almost completely cooked down, add the butter and sugar, lower the heat to medium low and continue to cook until reduced by half. Add the chocolate and stir until melted, taking care not to let the mixture boil.

4 Use the sauce to baste the ribs as they continue to cook – they will need 80-90 minutes in total until they are tender and cooked through.

RECOMMENDED BEER

There is big flavour and not a lot of spice in these ribs, so match it with a dark weizenbock that has bold and spicy flavours to match the meat, but also sufficient spritz to cut through the fattiness of the pork.

GREG HIGGINS

NORTHWEST BEER ADVENTURER

HIGGINS RESTAURANT, PORTLAND, OREGON, USA

PORTLAND, OREGON, IS NOT A CITY THAT IS HURTING FOR EITHER GREAT BREWERIES OR FINE RESTAURANTS. IT IS OFTEN SAID THAT THERE EXIST MORE OF THE FORMER PER CAPITA IN THE ROSE CITY THAN ANYWHERE ELSE IN THE WORLD, WHICH MAY OR MAY NOT BE TRUE, BUT IS UTTERLY BELIEVABLE EVEN IF IT IS NOT. AND THE TEMPTATION IS TO MAKE THE SAME CLAIM ABOUT RESTAURANTS.

Even amid such gastronomic bounty, however, Higgins Restaurant manages to stand out. Opened in 1994, its chef-owner, Greg Higgins, was one of the pioneers in emphasizing the bounty of the Pacific Northwest on his menu, a philosophy he brought with him from his previous employment at the city's Heathman Hotel. At least a decade before the practice became commonplace among chefs in North America, Higgins would go out of his way to form close relationships with local farmers, ranchers and fishermen.

'YOU CAN'T REALLY HELP BEING INFLUENCED BY THE AVAILABILITY AND DIVERSITY OF CRAFT BREWS (IN THE PORTLAND AREA), WHETHER AS A CHEF OR A DINER'

What's more, Greg wasn't about to ignore the wealth of beer choices on his front doorstep, choosing from the outset to give equal play to beer and wine. 'I can't really imagine our regional ingredients being separate from the brews', he says, 'Waverly Root said that where there's good wine, there's good food and I think the same is true of craft brews and food. A region that recognizes and supports great cuisine should and will do the same for all quality fermented beverages'.

Although Higgins Restaurant opened with a beer list long on Belgian brews – itself an irregularity for a fine dining restaurant at the time – it didn't take long for local craft beers to begin dominating the list. 'You can't really help being influenced by the availability and diversity of craft brews (in the Portland area), whether as a chef or a diner', says Higgins.

Indeed, while it is now quite common to find local craft beer in Portland's finer restaurants, when I first paid a visit to Higgins in the late 1990s, it stood out for both the high quality of cuisine and the fact that you could get a pint of Oregon IPA as easily as you could a glass of local pinot noir.

At least partial credit for that goes to Warren Steenson, Higgins Restaurant's former 'beer guy' and someone the chef credits with having been a 'huge influence'. He sadly passed away in 2014. For years at Higgins, Steenson was the fellow who would advise diners on beer and food pairing.

'Warren and I first worked together at the Heathman Hotel when I was the chef there', recounts Greg, 'He inspired me to do some brewing and coached me along in that process. Warren had a tremendous palate as well as a boundless appetite for brew knowledge (which) he shared with our staff and our clientele and I think was a catalyst in helping lead the local craft brew scene to where it is today. We really miss him...'

Among the many things Greg says he learned from Warren, local brewery owner Alan Sprints and a good friend, Jim Kennedy, owner of Admiralty Beverages, were the essentials of matching beer and food. 'It all comes down to stressing the basic ideas – bitterness, acidity, maltiness, sweetness and yeasty character and what to pair those to or against', he says.

OPPOSITE In the beer nirvana that is Portland, Oregon, Greg Higgins is chef-owner at Higgins Restaurant, where he specializes in creating dishes that pair local beer with local food.

CITRUS AND HAZELNUT CRUSTED HALIBUT WITH BIÈRE BLANCHE SAUCE

WHILE IT MIGHT APPEAR TO BE OVERLY INVOLVED, THIS FISH DISH FROM GREG HIGGINS OF HIGGINS RESTAURANT IN PORTLAND, OREGON, IS IN FACT RELATIVELY SIMPLE AND WORTH EVERY ONE OF THE STEPS IT TAKES TO COMPLETE.

SERVES 4

1 orange, zest and juice
1 lemon, zest and juice
120ml (4fl oz) Belgian-style wheat beer
4 shallots, finely chopped

1 tsp peppercorns
2 sprigs fresh thyme
1 tbsp ground coriander
½ tsp cayenne pepper
60g (2oz) hazelnuts,

toasted and crushed
salt and pepper to taste
1 egg white
1 tbsp Dijon mustard
25g (1oz) olive oil

4 × 170g (6oz) portions halibut
170g (6 oz) unsalted butter, cut into 1.25cm (½in) cubes

METHOD

1 Preheat the oven to 200°C/400° F/gas mark 6.

2 In a small non-reactive saucepan combine the orange juice, lemon juice, wheat beer, shallots, peppercorns, thyme and half of the cayenne and coriander. Bring to a boil then lower heat to simmer and allow to reduce to about 120ml (4fl oz) of liquid.

3 While the sauce reduces, chop the orange and lemon zest finely and combine it with the remaining coriander, cayenne and the hazelnuts. Season to taste with salt and pepper and set aside.

4 In a bowl, whisk together the egg white, the Dijon mustard and a dash of water. Season the halibut portions on both sides with salt and pepper and place them on a pan that you have thinly covered with olive oil. Lightly brush the top of each piece of halibut with the egg white mixture and then cover with the hazelnut crust. Roast until nicely browned, about 10–12 minutes.

5 While the fish cooks, check on the sauce reduction. When fully reduced, strain to remove the shallots and seasonings and return the liquid to the pan. Whisk in the butter and season to taste with salt and pepper.

6 Serve the crusted halibut and sauce with a tossed salad, a loaf of hearty bread and the remaining ale.

RECOMMENDED BEER

Given that all the main elements of a Belgian-style wheat beer already form part of this dish, it makes complete sense in this case to serve the dish with that same beer.

PAUL MERCURIO

BEER'S RENAISSANCE MAN

MORNINGTON, AUSTRALIA

IT WAS AT THE TENDER AGE OF 14 THAT PAUL MERCURIO MADE HIS TELEVISION CHEF DEBUT, APPEARING ON A CHILDREN'S TELEVISION SHOW IN HIS NATIVE AUSTRALIA TO PREPARE THE ULTIMATE 'JUST HOME FROM SCHOOL' SNACK. GIVEN HIS AGE AT THE TIME, HE'S QUICK TO POINT OUT THAT THERE WAS NO BEER INVOLVED!

Food, on the other hand, was an interest rapidly turning into a fascination for the young Mercurio, something that gestated through his work in food markets as a teen and exploded when his career as a dancer began to take him to locations from France to Korea, China to the United States. It was also during this time, he says, that his interest in the beer and food experience first developed.

'Often the beer wasn't all that good,' he recalls, 'But the total experience certainly was – think mussels in Brussels with a Stella or chops and a lager on top of a mountain in Greece!'

AFTER HIS WIFE BOUGHT HIM HIS FIRST HOMEBREWING KIT IN 1988, PAUL SAYS THAT HIS BEER AND FOOD 'JOURNEY' TRULY BEGAN. 'IN MAKING MY OWN BEER I REALISED THAT MAKING BEER WAS REALLY A COOKING PROCESS', HE SAYS, 'SO IT MADE COMPLETE SENSE TO NOT ONLY MATCH CERTAIN BEERS TO CERTAIN DISHES, BUT ALSO TO COOK WITH THE BEER'.

Although not classically trained in the culinary arts, Paul's high national profile as an acclaimed dancer, choreographer, actor and television personality, coupled with his genuine fascination with food and beer, has led him to author two cookbooks, including 2011's *Cooking with Beer*, a book he mailed to me by way of introduction in 2013. Impressed by the recipes contained within its pages, I resolved to find out more about its author, which led to a cyber-friendship with the man who describes himself as not a celebrity or a chef, but just 'a bloke who likes to cook'.

This sort of straightforward approach also colours Paul's advice for fellow cooks interested in bringing beer into their kitchen. 'First and foremost, do it!' he says, adding quickly that the best way to learn is from one's own successes and failures.

'Beyond that my top tip is this: if the dish you are cooking tastes like the beer you used in it, then you got it wrong,' says the dancer-turned-chef somewhat counter-intuitively, 'Beer is but one ingredient and should work harmoniously with all of the other ingredients. Sometimes you may want it to be a bit more upfront and sometimes you just want it to lay low in the background, so finding those subtleties is the fun part of cooking with beer'.

When it comes to the table, Paul is equally homespun. 'To me, it is probably the weather that is the influencing factor: seafood, barbeques, Asian influences and the beers that go with that style of eating in the summer – pilsners, hefeweizens, golden ales, saisons, etc. – while in the cooler months I tend to go more Mediterranean with risotto, one-pot dishes, slow cooking and the beers that go with that style of food – old ales, hoppy ambers, stouts, Belgian tripels and the like'.

Behind it all, however, Paul remains unabashedly a Down Under beer drinker, quick to also voice the opinion that there are no hard and fast rules to beer and food and that he is more than happy to enjoy a pilsner in winter or an Imperial stout in the summer.

'The best thing for me is how the Aussie way of life lends itself to good beer and good food shared with family and friends'.

OPPOSITE Having been introduced to and excited by the world of beer during his days as a dancer, Paul Mercurio made beer, food and cooking his second career.

MUSSELS IN COCONUT AND BEER

AUSTRALIAN CHEF PAUL MERCURIO SHARES MY GREAT AFFECTION FOR MUSSELS, AND OFFERS THE FOLLOWING HINT IN RELATION TO THIS DISH, WHICH I HAD NOT PREVIOUSLY CONSIDERED: IF THE MUSSELS ARE SUPER FRESH, THEY WILL BE FULL OF SEA WATER, WHICH MEANS THAT THE RESERVED COOKING LIQUID MAY BE SALTIER THAN YOU EXPECT. HE ADVISES TASTING IT AND REPLACING SOME WITH WATER IF YOU FIND THAT TO BE THE CASE. SERVE WITH PLENTY OF CRUSTY BREAD TO SOAK UP THE SAUCE.

SERVES 2 AS A MAIN COURSE OR 4 AS A STARTER

1 kg (2.2lb) fresh mussels
20g (¾oz) unsalted butter
2 tbsp olive oil
2 cloves garlic, chopped
1 small red chilli, finely chopped

1 long green chilli, thinly sliced
1 stick lemon grass
1 Lebanese/Asian or Chinese aubergine (long and thin), cut in half lengthways and sliced

2.5 cm (1in) piece of ginger, peeled
75g (2½oz) peas
6 kaffir lime leaves, stalk removed and thinly sliced
235ml (8fl oz) coconut milk

330ml (11fl oz) Belgian-style wheat beer
60ml (2fl oz) creamed coconut
1 tsp fish sauce
1 bunch fresh coriander, chopped

METHOD

1 Clean and de-beard the mussels discarding any with broken shells, set the rest aside in a colander.

2 In a pot large enough to hold the mussels on medium heat, add 1 tbsp oil. When the oil is hot, add half of the chopped garlic and the red chilli and cook for a minute or two, stirring and being careful not to burn the garlic. Turn the heat to high and add the mussels to the pot then one third of the bottle of beer. Put a lid on the pot and bring the beer to a boil. Cook the mussels until they are all open, approx 3–5 minutes, shaking the pot vigorously to tumble the mussels. Resist the urge to take a peek by lifting the lid, as you will let the steam out of the pot and slow down the cooking process.

3 When lots of steam starts to push its way through the lid, the mussels will be done. When all or most of the mussels have opened, remove pot from the heat and pour the mussels into a colander above a large mixing bowl to capture the cooking liquid.

4 Put the pot back on the heat, add the butter and 1 tablespoon of olive oil. When the butter foams, add the rest of the garlic and the green chilli and stir. With the flat of your kitchen knife or palm of your hand smash the peeled ginger so that it is squashed and falls into chunks. Add this to the pot. Peel away the tough outer layers of the lemon grass stalk to reveal the pale lower section of the stem. Use a sharp knife to trim the base. Cut the stalk into four pieces, then smash the stem with the flat side of a knife to bruise and release the flavour. Add to the pot. Add the aubergine to the pot along with the peas and the kaffir lime leaves. Stir well and cook until the aubergine has softened, about five minutes.

5 Add half of the remaining beer, the coconut milk, coconut cream and fish sauce and bring to the boil.

Remove the colander with the mussels from the large mixing bowl and set aside. Strain the cooking liquid from the mussels through a fine sieve to remove any dirt, grit or bits of shell and then add the liquor back into the pot, bring it to the boil, and turn the heat down a little so that it can simmer for a couple of minutes. Return the mussels to the pot and stir through so the hot liquid gets into the shells. Simmer for two minutes.

6   Divide the mussels and sauce equally into two large bowls and garnish with some freshly chopped coriander.

RECOMMENDED BEER

Pair with a mildly hoppy kölsch to balance the spiciness of the broth without overwhelming the flavour of the mussels.

DAVID MCMILLAN

FROM WINE TO BEER

MEDDLESOME MOTH, DALLAS, TEXAS, USA

AS THE CRAFT BEER MARKET SPREAD ACROSS THE UNITED STATES IN THE 1980S AND 1990S, IT CAUGHT ON IN SOME REGIONS LIKE THE PACIFIC NORTHWEST, NORTHERN CALIFORNIA AND LARGE PARTS OF NEW ENGLAND, MUCH MORE QUICKLY THAN IT DID IN OTHERS. AND ONE OF THE LAST AREAS TO EMBRACE THE MOVEMENT WAS THE AMERICAN SOUTH.

Bucking this resistance to beers of character was a small chain of bars called the Flying Saucer. Established early on in Texas, Arkansas and Tennessee, the Saucer group quickly earned a loyal following of aficionados they called 'beer knurds' and became recognized as the vanguard of craft beer in the south.

Entering the new century, the minds behind the Saucers, in particular resident beer wrangler Keith Schlabs, grew anxious to open up another frontier, one of sophisticated and elegant beer-oriented dining. The tool they used to accomplish this task was the Meddlesome Moth in Dallas, Texas, and the chef behind the kitchen was David McMillan.

From my first visit I was impressed with David's menus, which featured sophisticated takes on bar standards like burgers and pot pies during the day, while tending more towards brasserie fare such as steak tartare and sweetbreads at night. When I returned to host a beer dinner at the Moth a year or two later, impressed became enthralled.

Born and raised in Berkeley, California, David joined the Moth team as a consultant rather than the head chef because, as he recalls today, he was unsure the neighbourhood would support his unconventional effort. Thankfully, his doubts proved unfounded and he soon became a fixture in the Moth's kitchen.

Looking back, David says that the experience of joining the Moth was a bit like diving straight into the deep end of a pool. For while he had long been a beer drinker, his main culinary reference point was wine, with much of his

experience having been gained in France and northern California. He was dubious as to how it all would translate into beer but that concern, too, proved groundless.

'IT WAS QUITE A CHANGE, BUT I SOON FOUND THAT MY WINE BACKGROUND CAME IN QUITE HANDY', DAVID RECALLS, 'IT'S LIKE A MUSICIAN WHO CAN READ MUSIC, THEY UNDERSTAND IT REGARDLESS OF GENRE BECAUSE THE BASICS ARE PRETTY MUCH THE SAME'.

Pressed further, David allows that harmonies and contrasts can be similar whether the beverage is beer or wine, and that once you start tasting the various beer styles, you realize that their roles in the kitchen and at the table have strong parallels.

'The currently popular saisons and farmhouse style ales in particular tend to get pretty wine-like', he says, 'So I often use those as a sort of bridge to beer for wine drinkers. Once they accept the notion of comparable flavours, they tend to get drawn over to the beer side pretty quickly'.

In the kitchen, David says that as much as he enjoys cooking with beer, he also really likes using the ingredients of beer in his cuisine. Fortunate enough to have a large brewery supply store near his house, he says that he will often buy a bunch of different hops and grains and other ingredients to play around with in the kitchen, his latest favourite being malt syrups.

'I really like malt syrups for sauces and glazes,' he says, 'I'll create a base sauce with lots of herbs and such and blend it together with the malt syrup. The syrup can really bring a lot of depth'.

OPPOSITE David McMillan hard at work on one of his culinary creations at his Meddlesome Moth restaurant in Dallas, Texas.

BAY SCALLOPS WITH SWEET CORN & BARLEY WINE TAPIOCA

DAVID MCMILLAN OF THE MEDDLESOME MOTH IN DALLAS, TX, AND BIRD CAFÉ OF FORT WORTH, TX, OFFERS THIS SOPHISTICATED TAKE ON SOUTHERN COMFORT FOOD.

SERVES 4 AS A STARTER

1 ear of sweet corn
2 tsp + 1 tbsp butter
120ml (4fl oz) single cream
2 eggs, separated

2 tbsp sugar
2 tbsp quick-cooking
   tapioca
salt and white pepper

120ml (4fl oz) milk
120ml (4fl oz) soft barley
   wine
1 tsp vanilla

295g (10oz) bay (small)
   scallops, cleaned
Pale celery leaves from the
   heart

METHOD

1 Strip the kernels from the cob of corn and sauté them in a large pan with 2 tsp of butter. Transfer to a blender or food processor, add the single cream and purée, adding extra cream if necessary for consistency. Set aside.

2 In a separate bowl, beat the egg whites until foamy. Gradually add half the sugar, continuing to beat until stiff peaks form. Set aside.

3 In a medium-sized saucepan on medium heat, combine the rest of the sugar, the tapioca and the salt, mixing well. Stir in the milk, barley wine, vanilla and egg yolks. Cook over medium heat for 10–15 minutes or until mixture comes to a full boil, stirring constantly.

4 Remove the pan from the heat and fold the corn purée into the tapioca mixture. Gently fold in the egg whites until well blended. Reserve while still warm.

5 In a sauté pan on medium-high heat, melt 1 tablespoon butter. When it just begins to turn brown, add the scallops and spread them into a single layer. After 45 seconds shake pan to toss scallops and cook for one more minute. Season with salt and white pepper. Move the scallops immediately to a plate so they don't overcook and pour the butter and juice from the pan over the top.

6 To serve, spoon a generous amount of corn tapioca on to each of four serving plates, making a well in the centre of each mound. Divide the scallops between the plates, spooning them into the middle of the corn tapioca and covering with the juices. Sprinkle with celery leaf hearts and serve.

RECOMMENDED BEER

Pair this with a soft-bodied beer like a Belgian-style wheat beer.

ROASTED PUMPKIN AND STOUT GRITS

THIS DISH FROM DAVID MCMILLAN OF THE MEDDLESOME MOTH IN DALLAS, TX, AND BIRD CAFÉ OF FORT WORTH, TX, USES PUMPKIN, MILK STOUT AND CREAM TO BRING ADDED COMPLEXITY TO A STAPLE DISH OF THE DEEP SOUTH.

225g (8oz) pumpkin, roasted until soft then peeled and seeded

150g (5oz) grits or polenta
175ml (6fl oz) milk stout

480ml (16fl oz) water
double cream to taste

salt and pepper to taste

METHOD

1   In a food processor or with the back of a fork, purée the pumpkin. Set aside.
2   In a large pot on medium heat, combine the water and stout. When the liquid is hot but not boiling, stir in the grits.
3   Keep stirring continuously until the grits are smooth and creamy, adding extra water if necessary. Remove from the heat and fold in the pumpkin purée. Season to taste with salt and pepper and adjust the texture with double cream, adding very small amounts at a time. Return to the hob and keep warm until ready to serve.

RECOMMENDED BEER

As a side dish, you're unlikely to partner your beer directly with these grits, but if serving alongside grilled or roasted pork or beef, or some other richly flavourful meat, a spicy dubbel or spiced, malty ale could bring an additional harmonious flavour element to the table.

SALVATORE GAROFALO

ITALIAN BEER CUISINE ADVOCATE

LA RATERA, MILAN, ITALY

THE GROWTH OF CRAFT BEER IN ITALY HAS, SINCE DAY ONE, BEEN QUITE UNLIKE THE DEVELOPMENT OF THE CRAFT BEER SCENE ANYWHERE ELSE. RECOGNIZING THAT THEIR WINE-LOVING COUNTRYMEN MIGHT BE AT FIRST RELUCTANT TO EMBRACE FLAVOURS OUTSIDE OF THE STANDARDS SET BY THE BIG ITALIAN BREWERS – ESSENTIALLY PALE LAGER AND THE OCCASIONAL DOPPIO MALTO, OR LIGHTER BODIED DOPPELBOCK – EARLY ITALIAN CRAFT BREWERS CHOSE TO FOCUS UPON THE DINNER TABLE AS THEY DEVELOPED AND GREW THEIR NICHE.

This resulted in what is now viewed internationally as Italian craft beer's calling card: ornate bottles, food-friendly flavours and elegant glassware. What it rather curiously did not result in was a growth in the popularity of beer cuisine to rival that of *la birra artigianale*.

Unless, that is, you find yourself in Milan at the restaurant La Ratera. There, you will not only be able to order from an extensive list of characterful beers, but also you will be able to place your hunger in the very capable hands of Salvatore Garofalo.

Having honed his kitchen skills by working with many of Milan's top chefs, including Gualtiero Marchesi and Sergio Mei, among others, it was when Garofalo landed at La Ratera that he says his exploration into beer cuisine truly began.

'Prior to La Ratera, my experience with beer in the kitchen had been limited to a few dishes of my own, created because I already understood the potential of beer cuisine,' he recalls, 'But the turning point was when I met Marco Rinaldi, who was the owner of La Ratera at the time. Working together, we were able to not only create a menu that paired well with beer, but also adapt it so that it featured many dishes made with beer'.

So in-depth has been Salvatore's immersion into beer cuisine that he says when he now tastes a beer for the first time, he automatically thinks about how he might be able to use it in the kitchen. It is a commitment sufficiently in evidence that, when I asked him for beer cuisine suggestions in Italy, my Italian beer journalist friend Maurizio Maestrelli didn't hesitate to recommend La Ratera first and foremost.

'I believe that cooking with beer affords huge opportunity to the cook, greater even than wine when you consider the considerable differences between the various styles of beer', Garofalo says, 'Cooking with beer in my opinion is just the beginning of a journey that definitely will be long and fruitful'.

That said, the chef is also mindful of tradition when he's working in a restaurant kitchen, noting that certain dishes, such as *risotto alla Milanese* and *busecca*, belong not to the chef, but 'to history, to the memory of the people.' Those are the dishes he likes to leave unaltered on the menu, but elsewhere, Salvatore is far more carefree.

'I LOVE THE CONTRASTS THAT CAN BE HAD BY USING LAMBICS IN THE KITCHEN, RANGING FROM STARTERS TO THE PREPARATION OF WILD MEATS AND EVEN SPECIAL SWEETS,' HE ENTHUSES, 'WHEAT BEERS ALSO OFFER MANY OPPORTUNITIES, SUCH AS WHITE BEERS USED IN FISH DISHES, WEIZENBOCK FOR PORK AND HEFEWEIZEN FOR VEGETABLE SAUCES THAT GO WITH PASTA DISHES.'

OPPOSITE Salvatore Garofalo is so immersed in the world of beer cuisine that his first reaction on tasting a beer is to think about what kind of food it would work with.

SALTED COD WITH CLAM COUSCOUS

MILANESE CHEF SALVATORE GAROFALO WAS ONE OF THE FIRST IN ITALY TO EXPERIMENT WITH BEER CUISINE, BOTH AT THE TABLE AND IN HIS KITCHEN AT LA RATERA. THIS WONDERFUL COD AND CLAM RECIPE IS AMPLE EVIDENCE OF BOTH HIS SKILL AND ENTHUSIASM.

SERVES 4

800g (1¾lb) salted cod, soaked in several changes of water to remove the salt
½ kg (1lb) clams
olive oil

3 cloves garlic
1 small bunch parsley
a few leaves lemon thyme
500ml (17fl oz) Belgian-style wheat beer
100g (4oz) couscous

1 tsp garam masala
salt and pepper
1 leek, finely chopped
1 carrot, diced
half a red pepper, diced
half a yellow pepper, diced

1 courgette, diced
a few sprigs dill
extra virgin olive oil to taste

METHOD

1 Soak the clams for 2–3 hours in salted water then rinse well. Heat a pan large enough to hold all of the clams over medium heat and add the olive oil and garlic, sautéeing until fragrant. Add parsley and thyme and stir well, followed by the clams and 200ml (7 fl oz) of the beer. Cover and allow to steam until the clams open.

2 Remove the clams from the pan with a slotted spoon and allow to cool. Strain the cooking liquid through a fine sieve and set aside.

3 In a large bowl combine the couscous and the garam masala. Season with salt and pepper. Add 120ml (4fl oz) water and allow to stand for 10 minutes. Repeat. Then repeat a third time but with only 60ml (2 fl oz) water.

4 In a saucepan over medium-low heat, add 1 tsp of olive oil, the diced vegetables and a pinch of salt. Cover and cook until tender but still crunchy, about 5 minutes.

5 Steam the couscous for 5 minutes then place in a bowl with the cooked vegetables, cooking liquid from the clams and a dash of extra virgin olive oil. Mix well and keep warm.

6 Cut the fillet of cod into 12 slices and season.

7 Heat a pan large enough to hold the cod slices over medium heat and coat with olive oil. Add cod slices, the rest of the beer and the dill, cover and reduce the heat to medium low. When the cod is cooked, after about 5 minutes, add the clams and re-heat.

8 Place three cod slices and a quarter of the clams on top of the couscous in the centre of each plate and surround with three slices of cod and one quarter of the clams. Garnish with chopped herbs and a drizzle of olive oil.

RECOMMENDED BEER

A light-bodied porter would match well the clams and cod in this dish, but I think it might take a schwarzbier to bring all the flavours neatly together.

MITCHELL ADAMS

FOOD, BEER, CIDER AND PUBS

THE BULL, LONDON, ENGLAND

MITCH ADAMS FIRST DEVELOPED HIS FASCINATION WITH BEERS BEYOND THE BRITISH NORM AROUND 2004, WHEN HE FOUND HIMSELF EMPLOYED AT A PUB STOCKING BEERS FROM BELGIUM, GERMANY AND OTHER PARTS OF EUROPE, IN ADDITION TO CLASSIC BITTERS AND STOUTS. NOT LONG AFTER THAT, HE STUMBLED ONTO A BEER AND FOOD PAIRING EVENT AND, AS HE SAYS, 'THAT WAS IT!'.

Already sparked, his interest in matching beer and food turned into full flame when he began working at The Flask in Highgate, London, then run by Andrew Cooper, now proprietor of the Wild Beer Company.

'Andrew was way into (beer and food pairing), so we did quite a bit of it there', recalls Adams.

These days, Mitch is publican of The Bull, a brewery pub located about a half a mile from The Flask, but that is not to suggest that his transition from one to the other was a matter of a short stroll up the road.

'I worked elsewhere in between, most recently at the Thatchers Arms at Mount Bures', he tells me over a pint at The Bull, 'It's just a small village pub, but even there we were doing a number of beer dinners and tastings, probably four or five a year. Mostly it was locals who would attend, and while they might come out of curiosity, they usually left as believers'.

At The Bull, I notice that Mitch has gotten a bit loftier in his food and beer pairing ambitions, stocking between 60 and 70 different bottled beers from the UK, US, Belgium and beyond to complement the brewery's mostly traditional, British-style cask-conditioned ales. It is the latter that he recommends most often for the pub's more standard fare – fish and chips, rump steak and the like – but where the menu becomes more atypical, so do the beer selections.

'The fish dishes in particular pair quite well with a number of the Belgian beers we carry, and maybe some of the American ones, too', he says, 'But we do a lot of training so that the staff are able to suggest appropriate beers for all the different dishes, if that's what the customer wants'.

Even so, Mitch remains quite grounded in his approach to beer and food, opining that, in general, most beers will sit nicely alongside most meals. 'Although', he adds hastily,

'If you want something special, a true experience, you need them to line up together in some way'.

That 'way' can be according to the accepted guidelines that suggest certain beer styles as accompaniments for certain foods, or it can be what Mitch calls geographically or terroir-based pairings or even something more experiential.

'Sometimes you have cheese coming from the same company as beer, like with Chimay, or there is that beer you have on holiday that never tastes as good when you buy a bottle at home', he notes, 'The atmosphere, the environment is always going to make a difference in how a beer tastes, or how food tastes, for that matter'.

And sometimes that setting, be it place or ambiance or even music, will triumph over even the most skillfully crafted pairing.

OPPOSITE ABOVE LEFT AND RIGHT Ever since moving from Essex to London, Mitch Adams has made sure that The Bull is a destination pub for all those interested in great beer served with delicious and interesting food.

OPPOSITE BELOW The Bull is a bustling and busy pub in the heart of Highgate, London that boats a fine range of craft beers.

HOP 'HOT SMOKED' SALMON & BEER HOLLANDAISE

WITH MORE AND MORE PEOPLE OWNING STOVE-TOP SMOKERS, THIS DELICIOUS SALMON DISH FROM THE BULL PUB IN LONDON BECOMES A QUICK AND EASY WAY TO ADD A LITTLE HOPPINESS TO DINNER.

SERVES 2

For the salmon
30g (1oz) whole leaf hops*
3 Earl Grey tea bags

2 × 180g (6oz) salmon fillets
For the beer hollandaise
3 egg yolks

2 tsp white wine vinegar
200g (7oz) clarified butter

3 tbsp golden pale ale or
lightly hopped IPA

*Be sure to get the freshest whole leaf hops you can find, either from a friendly local brewer or a homebrew supply shop. Do not use hops from a natural food store, where they are sometimes sold for tea and can be often old and 'cheesy.' Citra or Cascade hops work very well.

METHOD

1 Preheat oven to 190°C/375°F/gas mark 5.
2 Remove loose tea from the tea bags and drop it into the bottom of a stove-top smoker, or a heavy-based pot you can cover with a steamer and a lid. Let it smoulder on a medium-high heat until it's smoking well. Add the hops then work quickly to introduce the salmon into the smoker.
3 Put the salmon fillets on parchment paper and place on the smoker tray or steamer. Cover with a lid, remove from the heat and allow to smoke for 2 minutes.
4 Transfer the salmon to a baking sheet and place in oven for 6–7 minutes or until firm but still moist. While the salmon is cooking, make the beer hollandaise.
5 In a double boiler over medium heat, or in a metal mixing bowl suspended over a pot of simmering water, whisk together the egg yolks, vinegar and beer until light and fluffy. Remove from heat and slowly whisk in clarified butter.
6 Serve the salmon filets with a generous pour of hollandaise on top.

RECOMMENDED BEER

Like most salmon, this dish pairs masterfully with dry or off-dry porter or stout, but you can add an extra degree of magic to the pairing by securing a not-too-roasty porter that has been hopped with the same hops you used to smoke the fish.

HOMEMADE BEER BAKED BEANS ON TOASTED SPENT-GRAIN MALT LOAF

BEANS ON TOAST IS A BRITISH FAVOURITE FOR A QUICK DINNER OR A SNACK, MADE EVEN MORE DELICIOUS IN THIS RECIPE FROM THE BULL PUB, MADE WITH SPENT GRAIN BREAD AND BEER-FLAVOURED BEANS.

SERVES 4 AS A MAIN DISH

Ingredients for bread
200ml (6 ½fl oz) warm water
200ml (6 ½fl oz) milk
20g (¾oz) yeast
60g (2oz) butter
90g (3oz) sugar

20g (¾oz) salt
230ml (7¾oz) apple juice
20g (½oz) malt extract
350g (12 ½ oz) spent grain*
230g (8oz) wholemeal flour
1kg (2.2lb) bread flour
1 egg, beaten

Ingredients for baked beans
1 × 400 ml (14oz) tin cannellini beans
1 × 400g (14oz) can butter beans
1 × 40og (14oz) can chopped tomatoes

1 tsp smoked paprika
200g (7oz) brown sugar
160ml (5 fl oz) red wine vinegar
240ml (8fl oz) dark, spiced ale (e.g. pumpkin ale)
oil for greasing bowl

*Spent grain is the leftover grain after the brewing process. Ask a friendly neighbourhood brewer if you can have a couple of cups, but let it dry out a bit before you weigh it for the recipe.

METHOD

FOR THE BREAD

1 Pour the warm water into a small mixing bowl, crumble in the yeast and let it dissolve.

2 In a saucepan over medium heat, combine the milk and butter and warm until the butter melts. Remove the pan from the heat and whisk in the sugar, salt, apple juice and malt extract.

3 Once the yeast has begun to bubble, combine it with the milk mixture into a mixing bowl. And the spent grain, reserving 2 tbsp, and add the wholemeal flour. Mix the dough, gradually adding the bread flour. Using a food mixer with a dough hook, continue mixing until the dough comes away from the sides of the bowl. Knead for 6–7 minutes.

4 When the dough is no longer sticky, transfer it to a separate bowl that has been coated with olive oil. Cover loosely with cling film or a moistened tea towel and leave to rise for 30-60 minutes until it has doubled in size.

5 Punch the dough back down to its original size and separate into two. Knead and shape into loaves.

6 Place the loaves on greased baking sheets and lightly brush with egg wash, sprinkling the remaining spent grain on top. Set aside until dough doubles in size.

7 Preheat the oven to 160°C/ 320°F/gas mark 3. Place baking sheets in the oven and bake for 45 minutes or until the loaves sound hollow when knocked on the bottoms. Remove from oven and allow to cool on a rack.

FOR THE BAKED BEANS

1 Preheat oven to 120°C/250° F/gas mark ½.

2 Combine all the ingredients in an oven-proof baking dish and mix well. Cover with a lid or tin foil and bake for approximately 3 hours, stirring occasionally and adding more beer if it looks to be getting too dry.

TO SERVE

1 Slice and toast the bread. Cover each slice with a generous helping of the beans. This is the sort of casual dish that you don't want to get too fussy over, and almost any beer will serve it well at the table.

RECOMMENDED BEER

While this dish will match well with most beers, if you want a sure-fire winner, try a pint of malty brown ale or porter with it.

... de lambics et les
dérivés

De Cam:
Lambiek Speciaal   5,6 %   75cl   26,5 €
Framboise Lambiek   6 %   75cl   28 €
Kriek Lambiek   6,5 %   75cl   28 €

Moriau: Oude geuze   7 %   75cl   18 €

Oud Beersel

Oude geuze   6 %   75cl   16,50 €
Oude kriek   6 %   75cl   18,00 €

Horal's Mega Blend (Toer de geuze 2013)

Oude geuze   7 %   75cl   30,00 €
bouteilles numérotées d'un mélange
de lambics des brasseries: Boon,
3 fonteinen, Timmermans, De Cam,
Oud Beersel, De Troch, Lindemans,
Hanssens & Tilquin

ALAIN FAYT

FLEMISH TRADITIONALIST WITH A TWIST

RESTOBIÈRES, BRUSSELS, BELGIUM

THE FIRST THING YOU NOTICE ON ENTERING RESTOBIÈRES, ALAIN FAYT'S BEER CUISINE-DEVOTED RESTAURANT IN SOUTH CENTRAL BRUSSELS, IS THE MASSIVE AMOUNT OF FOOD-THEMED BRIC-A-BRAC LINING THE WALLS AND CEILING, FROM ANTIQUE COCOA AND FLOUR TINS TO COLANDERS OF EVERY SIZE, SHAPE AND MATERIAL.

'This is history', explains the chef, gesturing to the rows of fading containers that once held bouillon, spices and speciality flours, 'This is important'.

To the chef whose twin passions are traditional *cuisine à la bière* and Flemish food culture, history certainly does matter, a fact that comes into evidence more clearly with every bite a diner takes at Restobières. Which is not to say that Alain's menu is hidebound and ancient. It is not. For while the chef is obviously passionate about things of the past, for him beer cuisine is 'an evolution'

BEER AND FOOD DESTINATION

'RESTOBIÈRES IN BRUSSELS WAS A WONDERFUL EXPERIENCE WHICH I CHERISH, AND HOPE TO EXPERIENCE AGAIN. IT WAS ABOUT THE BEER, THE FOOD, THE PEOPLE I WAS WITH, THE HOSPITALITY OF THE OWNER, AND HIS ENTERTAINMENT.'
LUKE NICHOLAS, OWNER OF EPIC BREWING, NEW ZEALAND

Chef Alain's personal evolution began in the late 1970s, when he says he began dreaming of a restaurant devoted to cooking and dining with beer. That dream became reality in 1982, when he opened the one-room predecessor of today's more sprawling Restobières and began serving customers by appointment only, while he simultaneously operated a growing catering business with a strong emphasis on Flemish culinary traditions. It was there that I first encountered Alain's creative take on beer cuisine, and marvelled at the enthusiasm he coupled with his obvious belief that creating great, flavourful dishes with beer was simply all in a day's work.

'We don't think of the "beer kitchen" here in Belgium', says Fayt, 'It is just something we do, it is automatic'.

That attitude is reflected in dishes like *waterzooi*, a creamy stew typical of the city of Ghent, which Fayt updates with a duck leg in place of the more common chicken or fish, and savoury country-style sausage spiced with the coriander-spiked Wallonian ale, La Chouffe.

'Beer is such a trend these days, everything is new, new, new,' Alain explains, 'But for me I like to cook with lambic and gueuze more than anything'.

Before recalling a lambic he once received in the kitchen that was so good 'none went in the food, every drop was in my glass,' Alain explains that the tastes of Flemish cuisine, sugar and vinegar, make the usually acidic lambic a natural for Belgian cuisine. 'The beers of today can be so bitter, it is difficult to use them because you need to worry about reduction, about flavours becoming too bitter,' he says, referring in particular to the IPAs that are rapidly becoming a forceful presence even in traditionally malty beer-focused Belgium, 'With lambic and gueuze, that is never a problem'.

OPPOSITE ABOVE One of the best and dominant features of Alain Fayt's restaurant Restobières in Brussels, Belgium is the sheer volume of food and beer paraphernalia.

OPPOSITE BELOW Ever the collector, Fayt's has grouped Belgian beer bottles on shelves across the windows, where they reflect light into one of the dining areas.

CARBONNADES DE BOEUF À LA FLAMANDE

SINCE EVERYONE KNOWS THAT STEWS IMPROVE WITH AGE, ALAIN FAYT, CHEF AND OWNER OF RESTOBIÈRES IN BRUSSELS, BELGIUM, SUGGESTS MAKING THIS A DAY AHEAD OF WHEN YOU PLAN TO SERVE IT, WHICH WOULD MEAN BEGINNING THE MARINADE TWO DAYS IN ADVANCE. HE PROBABLY HAS A POINT.

SERVES 8

2.5 kg (5½lb) beef cheeks
4 × 330ml (11fl oz) bottles Flemish red ale

1 bouquet garni (thyme, basil, rosemary and bay leaves tied in a bundle)

450g (1lb) onions, chopped
1 L (1 qt) veal stock
120ml (4fl oz) vinegar

8 tbsp mustard
100g (3½oz) slice gingerbread, crumbled

METHOD

1   The day before serving, cut the beef cheeks into pieces about 4cm (1 ½in) square and place in a bowl along with three quarters of the beer – three out of four 330ml (11fl oz) bottles – and the bouquet garni. Cover and refrigerate overnight.

2   In a large pan, sauté the onions in oil or butter until brown, remove and set aside. In the same pan with a little more oil or butter, brown all the pieces of beef cheek until brown, working in batches so they do not get too crowded and begin to steam, rather than brown. Remove and set aside.

3   In a large casserole on a medium heat, add the beef, onions, veal stock, vinegar, mustard, gingerbread slices and the remaining bottle of beer. Stir until combined and bring to a boil. Reduce to a simmer and cook for at least 90 minutes.

RECOMMENDED BEER

The presence of sweet and tart, spicy and savoury flavour combinations in this dish call for a beer with similar complexity. Here, try a Flemish red ale, the same beer style used in the cooking. (A Flemish brown would certainly do as well.)

MARTIN BOSLEY
CRAFT BEER CONVERT

BOSLEYSPANTRY.CO.NZ
WELLINGTON, NEW ZEALAND

LIKE MANY CULINARY PROFESSIONALS, MARTIN BOSLEY, ONE OF NEW ZEALAND'S FINEST AND MOST AWARDED CHEFS, STARTED YOUNG AND WORKED HIS WAY UP THROUGH THE RANKS OF THE RESTAURANT KITCHEN, TRAVELLING ABROAD ON OCCASION BUT ALWAYS RETURNING TO HIS HOME CITY OF WELLINGTON. THROUGH IT ALL HE, BY HIS OWN ADMISSION, SPENT MANY YEARS EXPLORING THE RELATIONSHIP BETWEEN WINE AND FOOD, WHILE IGNORING THE ONE BETWEEN BEER AND FOOD. IT TOOK THE INFLUENCE OF ONE OF NEW ZEALAND'S TOP BEER WRITERS TO GET HIM TO CHANGE HIS WAYS.

'I have Neil Miller to thank for introducing me to the kaleidoscopic range of flavours and potential that craft beer offered me,' says the chef. 'A sceptic at first, Tuatara Ardennes – a strong and spicy golden ale by a Wellington-area brewery – was my epiphany beer. I had no idea beer could taste as complex, as balanced, or be as mouth-fillingly delicious as that'.

Once made aware, however, Martin took to beer with enthusiasm, using it, as he had wine, as both an ingredient and an accompaniment. Of the former use, he says he is now as likely to reach for a bottle of beer or cider while cooking as he is a bottle of wine, frequently employing beer in place of stock. The complexity of flavours inherent in beer, he says, adds much in the way of body and depth to many dishes, both in the kitchen and at the table.

Testament to Martin's beer enthusiasm is the way we met in New Zealand: At a beer dinner I was hosting in Wellington. Jet-lagged and a bit bleary at the time, it was not for a day or two that the significance of one of the country's best-regarded chefs making time for a humble beer dinner truly dawned on me.

'BEER NOW MERITS MUCH CONSIDERATION, AND THE MATCHING OF BEER TO FOOD WITHIN THE STRUCTURE OF MY DEGUSTATION MENUS HAS BEEN AN EXCITING DEVELOPMENT', MARTIN EXPLAINED TO ME LATER, 'FREQUENTLY I FIND A BEER TO BE A MORE SUITABLE MATCH THAN A WINE. THIS NO LONGER SURPRISES ME.'

What's more, he insists that he is not the only chef in New Zealand to arrive at such an understanding and that, in fact, it is increasingly becoming the expected norm.

'There is a greater acceptance of drinking a beer with your fine-dining meal in New Zealand (than in other countries), and a sommelier will know as much about the beer list as the wine list and be able to recommend a suitable match', Martin maintains, 'But more importantly, the consumer expects a quality beer list and their knowledge is not to be underestimated'.

This obviously ties in well with the culinary leanings of a chef who describes himself as being 'unequivocally committed to New Zealand's food culture', given that New Zealand boasts a thriving and still-growing craft beer culture which, in some ways, dwarfs that of their much larger Australian neighbour. But it does present some challenges for someone who, like Bosley, often specializes in the fruits of the sea.

'With seafood, the subtleties of the ingredients can be dominated by anything too hoppy,' he explains, 'But generally I find that the darker the beer, the more food-friendly. I've also recently begun playing with sour beers, as I think they offer interesting food matching opportunities.'

OPPOSITE Martin Bosley, based in Wellington, New Zealand is a firm advocate of cooking with beer, using it as an ingredient in, and an accompaniment to, food.

TAGINE OF LAMB

WHILE THE LIST OF INGREDIENTS MIGHT SEEM A BIT OVERWHELMING, CHEF MARTIN BOSLEY'S BEER-FUELLED TAKE ON A TAGINE IS ACTUALLY QUITE A SIMPLE RECIPE AND PERFECT FOR WHEN YOU'RE ENTERTAINING, SINCE ALL THE WORK IS DONE WELL AHEAD OF TIME.

SERVES 6

1 tsp ground black pepper
1 ½ tbsp sweet paprika
1 tsp ground cumin
1 tsp ground coriander
1 ½ tbsp ground ginger
1 tbsp turmeric
2 tbsp ground cinnamon

1.6 kg (3.5 lb) (approx) boned shoulder of lamb, cut into 5cm (2 in) chunks
2 tbsp olive oil
1 large onion, sliced finely
2 cloves of garlic, crushed

500ml (17fl oz) tomato juice
1 × 400g (14oz) tin chopped tomatoes
120g (4oz) dried apricots
6 dates, chopped
2 tbsp sultanas
45g (1½ oz) flaked almonds

1 tsp saffron threads
600ml (20fl oz) traditional pale ale
2 tbsp parsley, chopped
Couscous to serve

METHOD

1   Pre heat the oven to 150°C/300°F/gas mark 2. Combine the pepper, paprika, cumin, coriander, ginger and turmeric and cinnamon in a bowl. Use half the mixture to coat the lamb, then cover it and leave to marinate overnight in the fridge.

2   In a deep casserole pan on medium heat, heat one tablespoon of the olive oil and add the onion, cooking until softened. In a separate frying pan, heat the remaining oil and sauté the lamb pieces, browning on all sides. Add the remaining spice mix to the onions and cook until fragrant, about 1 minute. Add the garlic to the onion mixture and sauté briefly.

3   Add the lamb to the onion mixture and mix. Pour 250ml (8½ fl oz) cup of tomato juice into the pan that held the lamb and bring to a simmer, scraping up any pan stickings, and pour these juices over the lamb. Add the remaining tomato juice, chopped tomatoes, apricots, dates, sultanas, almond flakes, saffron and beer. Bring to a lazy simmer, cover with a tight-fitting lid and bake in the oven for 2–2 ½ hours. Remove from the oven, sprinkle on the parsley and serve with couscous.

RECOMMENDED BEER

Lamb and Scotch ale is always a smart pairing, and in this case the ale's straightforward maltiness will also provide a palate-pleasing contrast to the spiciness of the dish.

LAMB SHANKS BRAISED IN PORTER WITH FRESH THYME

BACK IN THE MID 1990S, THIS RECIPE FROM CHEF LESLIE DILLON, THEN WITH THE PYRAMID ALEHOUSE IN SEATTLE, WASHINGTON, WAS ENOUGH TO CONVINCE ME IN PERPETUITY OF THE WISDOM OF BRAISING IN BEER.

SERVES 4

2 tbsp olive oil
4 lamb shanks
salt and pepper
2 tsp minced garlic

225g (8oz) onion, chopped
150g (5oz) carrot, finely
    chopped
150g (5oz) celery, chopped

150g (5oz) tomato, seeded
    and finely chopped
177ml (6fl oz) porter
2 bay leaves

300ml (10fl oz)beef stock
1 tsp salt
I tbsp fresh thyme, minced

METHOD

1   In a pan with a lid large enough to hold all four shanks, heat the olive oil on medium. Season the meat with salt and pepper and brown in the oil on all sides. Remove and set aside.

2   Add the onion, carrot and celery and sauté until the onion is translucent, about 3–4 minutes. Add the tomato and garlic and stir well. Use the porter to deglaze the pan, scraping up all the bits of stuck lamb, and then add the beef stock, bay leaves, salt and thyme and stir well. Return the shanks to the pan and bring the liquid to a boil.

3   Once boiling, reduce to a simmer and let braise until the lamb is tender, about 2–2½ hours, adding water or more beer if the liquid seems to be getting low.

RECOMMENDED BEER

When I first published this recipe, I recommended serving a 'strong, malty ale' alongside the dish, without specifying the style. I believe I was thinking of something along the lines of an old ale or perhaps a Scotch ale, and I think I was right.

MARK DORBER

EARLY ENGLISH BEER CUISINE ADVOCATE

THE ANCHOR, WALBERSWICK, SUFFOLK, ENGLAND

HAVING ABANDONED A CAREER IN THE FINANCIAL DISTRICT OF LONDON, MARK DORBER RAN THE ICONIC PUB THE WHITE HORSE IN PARSON'S GREEN, LONDON DURING THE 1990S AND WAS RESPONSIBLE FOR INTRODUCING THE CONCEPT OF BEER AND FOOD TO A DISCERNING CUSTOMER BASE OF FOOD AND BEER LOVERS. NOW HE IS FIRMLY ESTABLISHED AT THE ANCHOR IN THE BRITISH SUFFOLK COASTAL TOWN OF WALBERSWICK, WHERE HE CONTINUES TO THRIVE.

By the time I first visited the White Horse on Parson's Green in the late 1990s, it was far from the sketchy 'haunt of Fulham's petty criminals' that it apparently had been in the early 1980s. One of the architects of the transformation that occured at the now-landmark London beer pub was Mark Dorber, the man responsible for that rather unappealing descripton of the pub's former customers.

Having started his life at the 'Sloney Pony' during a vacation job in 1981, Mark, and landlady Sally Cruickshank, used good beer as a means to dissuade the patronage of the area's unsavoury characters and encourage the return of a more sophisticated clientele. As a pub rehabilitation strategy, it was as revolutionary as it was effective.

'We hosted the first ever Old Ale Festival in November of 1982 to great local acclaim,' Mark recounts, 'And followed up with a series of Mild, Burton Pale Ale, Porter & Stout and regional festivals in the 80s and early 90s.

The strategy worked, with the pub earning its first mention in the CAMRA Good Beer Guide in 1983 and, thanks to Mark's work on the wine list, winning the prestigious London Wine Pub of the Year award in 1987 and 1988. By 1990, Mark's lifelong interest in food and cooking had motivated him to work on improving the victual side of operations.

'Inspired by the work of Michael Jackson, we put on some limited *cuisine à la bière* menus and got some press interest from 1992', Mark says, adding that when Sally Cruickshank retired in 1995 they made the decision to also offer table service throughout the pub, in direct opposition to the then-emerging class of English gastropubs. By that point, he recalls, 'We had a wine- and beer-matched menu, a good, tight selection of mainly Belgian bottled beers, a growing range of imported draughts and a great range of permanent cask ales'.

Eventually Mark departed the White Horse to set up the Anchor pub with his wife Sophie in Suffolk. Here the couple display their devotion to fine beer, wine and food. Mark says that in the modern pub era an emphasis on cuisine is more important than ever.

'In the period since the global financial crash, beer volumes and profitability on all pub activities have been shrinking, (so) to attract clientele and especially for the rural market, it has to be the main focus of attention,' he insists.

And to partner with the pub's highly regarded cuisine, Mark stocks a wide range of draught, cask and bottled beers – highly impressive for a coastal pub.

'GUEUZE AND OTHER INTENTIONALLY SOUR BEERS ARE ENHANCED BY RICH, FATTY CHARCUTERIE, SMOKED BEERS SHOW DIFFERENT FACETS WITH THE FOIL OF SLOW-COOKED PORK AND HEAVILY ROASTED STOUTS AND IMPERIAL STOUTS ARE IMPROVED BY BEING PAIRED WITH BROWNED AND CHAR-GRILLED RED MEATS'.

As for those often-overlooked beer styles of the British Empire, ales designed more for quaffing, Mark has ideas. 'Historic "session beers" brewed at reduced gravities tend to build flavour pint by pint in the perception of the drinker,' he observes, 'But the subtler flavour of lighter milds and session bitters work well with fish and chips or a clean crisp bitter pairs well with a 6-month-old cheddar ploughman's lunch, sausage rolls or a not too peppery pork pies. Their job is to cleanse and refresh, as well as provide contrast and the odd flavour hook'.

RÖSTI POTATO WITH WILTED KALE, GOAT CHEESE AND BEER BEURRE BLANC

ALTHOUGH THIS DISH FROM THE ANCHOR PUB MIGHT SEEM COMPLICATED, IT IS ACTUALLY JUST A NUMBER OF FAIRLY SIMPLE STEPS THAT RESULTS IN A DELICIOUS AND QUITE ATTRACTIVE APPETIZER OR SIDE DISH.

SERVES 4

For the rösti
2 large potatoes, floury in
    texture (e.g.russet)
¼ large Spanish onion,
    thinly sliced
a sprig of thyme
salt and black pepper to taste
clarified butter or duck fat
    for frying

For the kale
1 bunch kale, stalks
    removed and roughly
    chopped

For the beer beurre blanc
1 long shallot, peeled and
    finely chopped
sunflower oil for frying
1 garlic clove, peeled and
    finely chopped
240ml (8fl oz) saison (they
    use Saison Dupont at
    the Anchor)

120ml (4 fl oz) white
    wine vinegar
225g (8oz) cold unsalted
    butter cut into 1cm
    (½in) cubes
sea salt and ground white
    pepper to taste
1 slice goat's cheese

METHOD

FOR THE RÖSTI

1 Grate the potatoes coarsely into the a clean tea towel. Fold the towel around the potato to form a ball and squeeze to remove as much moisture as possible. Tip into a large bowl.

2 Sauté onions in a couple of tablespoons of clarified butter until soft and add to the potato along with thyme leaves and seasoning, Mix well.

3 Heat a large frying pan over a medium heat and add two tablespoons of the clarified butter or duck fat. Place a metal chef's ring inside the frying pan and fill carefully with one-quarter of the potato mix. Using the back of a spoon gently push down to make a compact cake. Remove the ring and repeat with the remaining potato until you have four rösti.

4 Fry the rösti for 3–4 minutes on both sides, or until golden-brown all over and tender all the way through, adding more oil or fat if required. Remove from the pan and drain on kitchen paper, adjusting the seasoning if necessary. Place onto a roasting tray and reheat before serving.

FOR THE KALE

1 In a large pot of boiling water, add the kale and let wilt for a minute or two. Remove from heat, drain and plunge kale immediately into cold water to stop cooking. Rinse and set aside for later.

FOR THE BEURRE BLANC

1 In a saucepan on medium heat, soften the shallot in a small amount of oil but do not brown. Add the garlic and cook for another minute. Add in the beer and vinegar, bring to a rapid boil and reduce down to 2–3 tablespoons in volume.

2 Turn heat to low and whisk in butter, melting in a cube at a time. Do not allow to boil. When a thick cream has formed, season to taste and keep warm for use.

TO SERVE

1 Reheat the rösti on a baking sheet in the oven. Remove, top with some kale and a slice of goat's cheese. Place under broiler until the cheese browns and begins to melt. Place each rösti on a plate or soup bowl and surround with the beurre blanc. Top with onion relish if desired.

RECOMMENDED BEER

The richness of this dish lends itself to a contrasting beer character, in this case a crisp helles or, if a beer with more oomph is desired, a moderately hoppy tripel.

PRUNE AND CHOCOLATE BROWNIES

PRUNES MIGHT NOT BE THE FIRST INGREDIENT THAT COMES TO MIND WHEN CHOCOLATE BROWNIES ARE MENTIONED, BUT THE RICHNESS OF NEW ZEALAND CHEF MARTIN BOSLEY'S RECIPE IN WHICH THEY ARE COMBINED WITH RICH, MALTY ALE WILL QUICKLY MAKE YOU A CONVERT.

MAKES 12 SQUARES

75ml (2 ½fl oz) strong, Belgian-style dark ale

250g (9 oz) caster sugar

250g (9oz) pitted soft prunes

200g (7oz) butter

250g (9oz) dark chocolate

3 large eggs, plus 1 yolk

60g (2 ½ oz) plain flour

55g (2oz scant) cocoa powder

1tsp baking powder

METHOD

1   Preheat the oven to 180°C/350°F/gas mark 4. Grease and line a 20cm (8 in) square baking tin with parchment paper

2   Cut each prune in half and put in a bowl. Pour over the beer and leave for at least 30 minutes.

3   In a food mixer or a bowl with an electric beater, add the caster sugar and butter and beat thoroughly until pale and creamy. Set aside. Place a metal bowl over a pot of simmering water, or use a double boiler, and snap the chocolate into pieces and put them in the bowl. Leave the chocolate to melt, avoiding the temptation to stir, but taking care to ensure the chocolate doesn't cook. As soon as the chocolate becomes liquid, turn off the heat.

4   In a bowl. break the eggs, add the extra yolk and beat lightly with a fork. Into a separate bowl, sift the flour, cocoa and baking powder and set aside.

5   Returning to the mixer, or the bowl where the caster sugar and butter were beaten, add the beaten egg and, with the mixer on low speed, pour in the melted chocolate. Stop the machine when integrated and remove from mixing stand, if applicable. Drain the prunes of any excess liquid and add them to the butter-chocolate mixture. Then gently fold in the flour mixture, taking care not to over mix, or your brownie will be flat and heavy.

6   Scrape the mixture into the prepared cake tin and bake for 30 minutes. Remove from the oven and leave to cool before slicing into (at least) 12 squares.

RECOMMENDED BEER

Anything strong, dark and sweet would work well with this dish, but a highly malty abbey-style strong dark ale would be absolutely sublime.

BLUEBERRY RICOTTA BEIGNETS WITH STOUT CHOCOLATE SAUCE

THE ADDITION OF RICOTTA TO THESE BEIGNETS FROM AMERICAN COOKBOOK AUTHOR LUCY SAUNDERS ADDS A DELECTABLE LIGHTNESS, WHILE THE STOUT IN THE CHOCOLATE SAUCE ADDS FLAVOURSOME DEPTH TO THE DIPPING SAUCE.

MAKES 12-15 BEIGNETS

For the beignets
2 large eggs
50g (2oz) sugar
225g (8oz) ricotta
1 tsp vanilla extract

pinch of salt
1 tbsp baking powder
110g (4oz) flour
grapeseed oil
50g (2oz) blueberries

For the sauce
225g (8oz) dark chocolate 60%, finely chopped
225g (8fl oz) double cream
120ml (4fl oz) Imperial stout

1 tsp vanilla extract (preferably Madagascar Bourbon Vanilla)

METHOD

BLUEBERRY RICOTTA BEIGNETS

1 Whisk together eggs, sugar, ricotta, vanilla, salt, baking powder and flour until smooth. Cover and refrigerate for 2 hours to let the batter rest.

2 Place a large heavy saucepan on the stove and add grapeseed oil to a depth of 6cm (2½in). Turn heat to medium-high and bring to 180°C/350°F, testing temperature with a thermometer.

3 To make the beignets, mix blueberries into the batter and drop by the tablespoonful into the hot oil and fry, turning once with tongs or a mesh spoon, to cook until browned well on both sides. Cook 4–6 beignets at one time, so the pan doesn't get too crowded. Stir batter before making new batch, so every beignet has several blueberries (otherwise, they will sink to the bottom of the batter). Cook about 2 minutes on each side. Replenish oil to a depth of 6cm (2 ½in) and allow oil to reheat to 180°C/350°F between batches.

4 Remove beignets and drain on paper towel or brown paper. Keep warm in oven until ready to serve. Serve warm with stout chocolate sauce.

STOUT CHOCOLATE SAUCE

5 Place the chopped chocolate in a mixing bowl. Mix cream and stout in a saucepan and bring to a simmer over a medium-high heat. Remove from heat, and pour over the chopped chocolate. Gently whisk until the chocolate melts and sauce is smooth. Whisk in the vanilla and serve warm, or cool completely and store in an airtight container in the refrigerator for up to a week, in which case reheat gently before serving.

RECOMMENDED BEER

While Lucy likes to pair these with a robust American amber ale or malty dark lager, my preference would be to reach for a Baltic porter or not-too-hoppy Imperial stout.

CHOCOLATE, BEETROOT AND STOUT CAKE

AUSTRALIAN CHEF AND TELEVISION PERSONALITY, PAUL MERCURIO, ADMITS THAT SOMETIMES HE GETS INTO A MOOD WHERE HE 'JUST CAN'T STOP THINKING ABOUT PUTTING A BUNCH OF INGREDIENTS TOGETHER THAT MAY, AT FIRST THOUGHT, BE A WEIRD IDEA'. HENCE THIS OFFBEAT CAKE WHICH, DESPITE ITS BEET CONTENT, IS QUITE DELICIOUS!

SERVES 10

1 large beetroot, approx 300g (11oz)

Juice of 1 large orange

150ml (5fl oz) strong stout in the 6.5% ABV or greater range (but not too sweet), carefully warmed to a simmer

230g (8oz) of self-raising flour

50g (2oz) cocoa powder

200g (7oz) brown sugar

Zest of one lemon

60g (2 ½oz) milk chocolate

60g (2 ½oz) 70% dark chocolate

100g (3½oz) unsalted butter, chopped

3 free range eggs, beaten

METHOD

1 Pre-heat oven to 160° C /320° F/gas mark 3).

2 Butter then line a 24cm (9in) springform cake tin with baking paper – bottom and sides.

3 Wash and trim the beetroot, cut in half and then cut each half in quarters. Place in a small saucepan with lid, add orange juice and gently simmer, with lid on, until just tender. Remove beetroot and place in a bowl with cold water. When cool enough to handle, remove the skin by gently scrapping with a knife and cut into small cubes. Place in a food processor and blitz until a paste forms. Add half of the stout, blitz some more, then set aside.

4 Sift flour and cocoa into a large bowl. Stir in the sugar and lemon zest and set aside.

5 Pour 300ml (10 fl oz) water into a saucepan or the bottom of a *bain marie* or double boiler and bring to the boil before reducing to a simmer. Chop the chocolate into small pieces and put in a bowl or the top portion of the double boiler and place over the simmering water. Allow the chocolate to melt before giving it a stir to combine. Add the chopped butter to the chocolate and allow it to melt before stirring to combine. Remove the bowl from the saucepan and allow the mix to cool a little before adding the three beaten eggs and then the rest of the warm stout and the beetroot purée, giving everything a good stir so it is well combined.

6 Pour the chocolate beetroot mix into the bowl with the dry ingredients and give it a good stir so there are no dry lumps, then pour into your prepared cake tin and pop that in to the oven.

7 Cook for about 40 minutes. Check cake is done by inserting a wooden skewer into the cake – it should come out pretty clean or with just a few crumbs on it. If it comes out with wet cake mix, cook a little longer.

8 Allow cake to cool before turning out. Serve warm as is or put in the fridge to cool completely before icing.

CHOCOLATE STOUT ICING METHOD

250g (9oz) ounces icing sugar, sifted

80g (3oz) ounces unsalted butter, melted

60 ml(2 fl oz) Stout
40g (1 ½oz) milk chocolate, finely chopped

40g (1 ½oz) of dark chocolate 70%, finely chopped

METHOD

1. Put the butter, stout and chocolate in a saucepan over gentle heat and stir while it all melts then mix well together. Sift the flour into a bowl and then gradually whisk into the melted chocolate mixture until well combined and smooth. Remove from the heat and allow to cool before icing the cake.

2. After carefully icing the cake – the icing will run, so pour it carefully onto the centre of the cake and allow it to spread – put the cake in the refrigerator until the icing is set.

RECOMMENDED BEER

Dense, rich and very chocolatey, this cake is sturdy enough to stand up to the strongest of Imperial stouts, although a contrasting approach would be to cut the intensity with the spice and effervescence of a good weizenbock.

BEER AND FOOD PAIRING CHARTS

EGGS, BREAD AND PASTRIES

FOOD	PAIRS WITH...
Light egg dishes (scrambled, fried)	Hefeweizen, kölsch
Weightier egg dishes (omelettes, eggs Benedict)	Dunkelweizen, pilsner, standard bitter
Pancakes with maple syrup	Maple-flavoured beer, stout, sweet doppelbock
Quiche lorraine	Dunkel, helles, rauchbier
Fresh fruit parfait with yogurt and granola	Fruit wheat beer, Berliner weisse, Belgian-style wheat beer

FOOD	PAIRS WITH...
Huevos rancheros	Pilsner, American style pale ale
Churros, doughnuts	Sweet stout, Baltic porter, barley wine
Toast and jam	Fruit-flavoured ale, dunkelweizen
Continental brunch	Hefeweizen, oatmeal stout

ULTIMATE PARTNER	SUCH AS...
Belgian-style wheat beer	Blanche de Namur
Helles	Augustiner Edelstoff
Oatmeal stout	Rogue Shakespeare Oatmeal Stout
Altbier	Uerige Altbier
Dry fruit lambic	Cantillon Rosé de Gambrius

ULTIMATE PARTNER	SUCH AS...
Traditional-style IPA	Worthington White Shield
Chocolate stout	Young's Double Chocolate Stout
Brown ale	Samuel Smith Nut Brown Ale
Coffee-flavoured stout or porter	Meantime Coffee Porter

CHEESE DISHES

FOOD	PAIRS WITH...
Brie and other soft, bloomy rind cheeses	Dry stout, London porter
Soft and moist goat's milk cheese	Belgian-style wheat beer, golden ale
Edam and other mild, semi-soft cheeses	Dunkel, Scotch ale, dubbel
Aged Cheddar and other sharp and nutty cheeses	Porter, dry stout, best bitter
Parmigiano reggiano and other aged, crumbly cheeses	Brown ale, porter
Stilton and other mild to moderate blue cheeses	London porter, dubbel
Roquefort and other sharp blue cheeses	Double IPA, strong dark ale
Epoisses and other pungent, washed-rind cheeses	Weizenbock, Imperial stout
Sag paneer (fresh cheese in spinach sauce)	Amber lager, mild
Croque monsieur/grilled cheese sandwich	London porter, brown ale, saison
Ploughman's lunch (cheese, pickles, bread, chutney)	Porter, steam beer
Cured meats and cheeses	Pale ale, best bitter, dunkel

ULTIMATE PARTNER	SUCH AS...
Oatmeal stout	Rogue Shakespeare Oatmeal Stout
Hefeweizen	Schöfferhofer hefeweizen
Bock	Weltenburger Kloster Asam Bock
ESB	Fuller's ESB

ULTIMATE PARTNER	SUCH AS...
Bourbon barrel-aged porter or stout	Goose Island Bourbon County Stout
British-style barley wine	Ridgeway Imperial Barley Wine
American-style barley wine	Rogue Old Crustacean Barley Wine
Belgian-style spiced ale (the stronger, the better)	Delirium Tremens

ULTIMATE PARTNER	SUCH AS...
Dunkel	König Ludwig Dunkel
Belgian-style spiced ale (golden & fruity)	Augustijn blond
Best bitter	Tring Brewery Ridgeway Bitter
Czech-style pilsner	Budweiser Budvar

FISH AND SEAFOOD

FOOD	PAIRS WITH...
Smoked salmon	Dry and roasty stout or porter, hefeweizen
Deep-fried calamari	Czech-style pilsner, kölsch
Creamy seafood chowder	Czech-style pilsner, saison
Ceviche (raw fish cured in citrus juice)	Soft fruit lambic (eg. apricot), kölsch
Fish and chips	Traditional IPA, hoppy brown ale

FOOD	PAIRS WITH...
Snapper, sea bass or other light-weight fish	Wheat ale, hefeweizen
Cod, halibut and other firm and meaty fish	Helles, schwarzbier, London porter
Steamed mussels or clams	Pair with the cooking beer, or as a default...
Lobster, steamed with clarified butter	London porter, oatmeal stout
Salade Niçoise	Weizenbock, Belgian-style spiced ale

ULTIMATE PARTNER	SUCH AS...
Smoked malt porter or stout	Alaskan Smoked Porter
Altbier	Uerige Alt
Golden bitter	Hop Back Summer Lightning
Belgian-style wheat beer	Watou's Wit
Best bitter	Brakspear Bitter

Kristal weissbier	Maisel's Weisse Kristall
Golden ale	Adnam's Explorer
Belgian-style wheat beer	St Bernardus Wit
Brown ale	Samuel Smith's Nut Brown Ale
Hefeweizen	Weihenstephaner Hefe Weissbier

PASTA, PIZZA AND RICE

FOOD	PAIRS WITH...
Spaghetti bolognese	Vienna lager, amber ale
Gnocchi with pesto	Märzen, Czech-style lager
Fettucine carbonara	Saison, helles, dunkel
Penne arrabbiata	Vienna lager, bock
Pasta e fagioli (with beans)	Altbier, dunkel

FOOD	PAIRS WITH...
Pizza margherita	Bock, amber ale
Fully loaded pizza	Golden bitter, American-style or traditional pale ale
Risotto Milanese	Golden bitter, helles
Pad Thai	Golden bitter, German-style pilsner
Westernized Chinese food (fried rice, chow mein, etc.)	Traditional pale ale, Czech-style pilsner

ULTIMATE PARTNER	SUCH AS...
Bock	Monschof Bockbier
Helles	Camden Hells
Czech-style pilsner	Pilsner Urquell
Traditional pale ale	Timothy Taylor Landlord
Schwarzbier	Köstritzer

ULTIMATE PARTNER	SUCH AS...
Vienna lager	Brooklyn Lager
American style IPA	Founder's Centennial IPA
Kölsch	Gaffel Kölsch
Traditional pale ale	Hitachino Nest Beer Pale Ale
American-style pale ale	Flying Dog Pale Ale

BEEF AND PORK

FOOD	PAIRS WITH...
Chilli con carne	Traditional or American-style IPA, Traditional pale ale
Medium rare roast beef	Best bitter, porter
Carbonnade de boeuf (beef stew, cooked in dark ale)	Dubbel, strong brown ale
Steak frites	Scotch ale, dubbel
Steak tartare	Traditional pale ale, porter

FOOD	PAIRS WITH...
Braised beef cheeks	Old ale, Imperial stout
Hamburger	Czech-style pilsner, hoppy brown ale
Beef korma (mildly spicy cashew and cream sauce)	Scottish style ale, porter
Grilled pork chops	Helles, dunkel, doppelbock
Roast loin of pork	Dunkel, porter, brown ale

FOOD	PAIRS WITH...
Pulled pork	Märzen, traditional pale ale (if spicy)
Italian sausage	Hoppy brown ale, dunkel, traditional pale ale
Bratwurst	Helles lager, dunkel
Weisswurst	Belgian-style wheat beer, light wheat ale
Full English brunch	Best bitter, pale ale, pilsner

ULTIMATE PARTNER	SUCH AS...
American-style pale ale	Oskar Blue's Dale's Pale Ale
Brown ale	Anspach & Hobday The Smoked Brown
Flemish brown ale	Liefmans Goudenband
Extra special bitter	Fuller's ESB
Belgian-style spiced ale (dark & malty)	McChouffe

ULTIMATE PARTNER	SUCH AS...
Strong dark ale	Trappistes Rochefort 10
American-style pale ale	Sierra Nevada Pale Ale
Brown ale	Samuel Smith Nut Brown Ale
Bock	Andechs Bergbock Hell
Weizenbock	Weihenstephaner Vitus Weizenbock

ULTIMATE PARTNER	SUCH AS...
Bock	Ayinger Winter Bock
Traditional IPA	Shepherd Neame India Pale Ale
Märzen	Hofbräu Oktoberfestbier
Hefeweizen	Weihenstephaner Hefe Weissbier
Standard bitter	Fuller's Chiswick Bitter

CHICKEN, LAMB AND DUCK

FOOD	PAIRS WITH...
Spicy chicken wings	Traditional pale ale, Czech-style pilsner
Grilled chicken breasts with barbeque sauce	Czech-style pilsner, saison
General Tao's chicken	Steam beer, Belgian-style enkel
Kung pao chicken	Helles, kölsch
Chicken vindaloo (very spicy)	American-style pale ale or IPA
Butter chicken (mild curry)	Amber ale, schwarzbier
Peking duck	German-style pilsner, hefeweizen
Roast leg of lamb	Porter, strong dark ale, Baltic porter
Lamb rogan josh	Double IPA, Baltic porter
Goulash	Traditional pale ale, traditional IPA

ULTIMATE PARTNER	SUCH AS...
American-style pale ale	Sierra Nevada Pale Ale
Vienna lager	Brooklyn Lager
Belgian-style tripel	Westmalle Trappist Tripel
Golden bitter	Woodforde's Wherry
Traditional IPA	Thornbridge Jaipur IPA

ULTIMATE PARTNER	SUCH AS...
Dunkelweizen	Weihenstephaner Hefeweissbier Dunkel
Weizenbock	Schneider Aventinus
British-style barley wine	Woodforde's Head Cracker
British-style barley wine	Samuel Smith Yorkshire Stingo
American-style pale ale	Odell 5 Barrel Pale Ale

VEGETABLES

FOOD	PAIRS WITH...
Ratatouille	Schwarzbier, Vienna lager
Stuffed sweet peppers	Altbier, Berliner weisse
Macaroni and cheese	Traditional pale ale, traditional IPA
Grilled portobello mushrooms	Dry stout, dunkel, mild

FOOD	PAIRS WITH...
Roasted root vegetables	Helles, best bitter
Channa masala (chick peas with tomato, onion)	Vienna lager, altbier
Caesar salad	Berliner weisse, gueuze
French onion soup	Flemish brown ale, brown ale

DESSERT

FOOD	PAIRS WITH...
Cheesecake with fruit topping	Belgian-style wheat beer, Scotch ale
Chocolate cake	British-style barley wine, New World spiced beer (porter)
Pumpkin pie	Pumpkin beer, bock
Christmas pudding	British-style barley wine, old ale
Apple pie	Fruited ale, eisbock, weizenbock
Trifle	Baltic porter, whisky barrel-aged porter

ULTIMATE PARTNER	SUCH AS...
Bock	Weltenburger Kloster Asam Bock
Traditional pale ale	Marston's Pedigree
Brown ale	Samuel Smith Nut Brown Ale
Schwarzbier	Würzburger Hofbräu Schwarzbier
Golden bitter	Coniston Bluebird Bitter
Brown ale	Anspach & Hobday The Smoked Brown
German-style pilsner	Jever Pilsner
Best bitter	Adnams Broadside

Fruited ale	Meantime Raspberry
Imperial stout	The Kernel Imperial Brown Stout
Brown ale	Brooklyn Brown Ale
New World spiced beer (strong)	Jolly Pumpkin Maracaibo Especial
New World spiced beer (mild)	Hop Back Taiphoon Lemon Grass
Scotch ale	Traquair House Ale

BEER AND FOOD PAIRING

BEER STYLE	SUCH AS
Traditional pale ale/best bitter	Fuller's London Pride
Blonde/golden bitter	Hop Back Summer Lightning
American-style pale ale	Sierra Nevada Pale Ale
Traditional India pale ale	Meantime India Pale Ale
American-style India Pale Ale	Oakham Ales Green Devil
Double or Imperial IPA	Russian River Pliny the Elder
Saison	Saison Dupont
Czech- or Bohemian-style pilsner	Pilsner Urquell
German-style pilsner	Bitburger
Kölsch/Golden/Blonde Ale	Gaffel Kölsch
Belgian-style tripel	Westmalle Tripel
Steam beer	Anchor Steam Beer
Helles	Augustiner Edelstoff
Märzen/Oktoberfest	Hofbräu Oktoberfestbier

GOOD WITH	PERFECT WITH
Fish and chips, pork pies, medium roast beef	Well-aged Cheddar cheese
Cream soups, spicy chicken and fish dishes	Shrimp and vegetable tempura
Spicy chillis, nachos, oily stir frys	Cheeseburger
Spicy meat stews, samosas and other deep-fried snacks	Spicy curry
Deep-fried pub fare, spicy tacos and buritos	Fully loaded, Chicago-style deep dish pizza
Mole sauced dishes, rich Indian dishes	80% or greater cocoa content chocolate
Most Thai and Vietnamese dishes, nutty cheeses	Rijsttafel (a collection of small dishes of Indonesian origin)
French fries, fettuccine alfredo, dumplings	Blackened catfish
Rich cream soups, chicken wings, Portuguese churrasco	Mixed grill (sausages, chops, chicken breast)
Pork tenderloin, firm flesh fish, Waldorf salad	Grilled pork chops
Pungent soft cheeses, gratin of Belgian endive	Asparagus with hollandaise sauce
Italian sausages, charcuterie	Ciopinno (tomato, fennel and seafood stew)
Roast chicken, roast pork loin	Doughy pretzels with mustard
Roast pork knuckle, chicken salad	Pork sausage

BEER AND FOOD PAIRING

BEER STYLE	SUCH AS
Vienna lager	Samuel Adams Boston Lager
Mild ale	Rudgates Ruby Mild
Brown ale	Samuel Smith Nut Brown Ale
Scottish-style ale	Belhaven 80/-
Hoppy brown ale	Brooklyn Brown Ale
Altbier	Uerige Altbier
Dunkel lager	Ayinger Altbairisch Dunkel
Schwarzbier	Köstritzer
Porter	Porterhouse Plain Porter
Baltic porter	Les Trois Mosquetaires Porter Baltique
Dry stout	Wrasslers 4X Stout
Oatmeal stout	Fourpure Oatmeal Stout
Imperial stout	Samuel Smith Imperial Stout
Rauchbier/Other smoked malt beers	Aecht Schlenkerla Rauchbier Märzen

GOOD WITH	PERFECT WITH
Pastas in tomato sauce, mild cheeses	Pizza margherita
Mildly flavoured beef stews, baked eggs (oeufs en cocotte)	Fricassée of mushrooms
Beef cooked to medium or more, roasted nuts	Liver and onions
Smoked mackerel, beef stroganoff	Scotch egg
Texas barbecue brisket, macaroni and cheeses	Braised beef short ribs
Firm and nutty cheeses, braised meats	Spiced sausage on dark rye bread
Beef sausage, roasted pork, root vegetables	Schnitzel with mushroom sauce
Sauerbraten, dim sum, mushroom dishes	Boudin noir (black pudding)
Steamed clams, oysters, cured or smoked fish	Smoked salmon on soda bread
Vegetable stews, trifle and other fruity desserts	Tiramisu
Lamb stew, venison, smoked fish	Oysters on the half-shell
Most breakfast foods (esp. oatmeal), chilled shellfish	Brie de Meaux
High cocoa content chocolate, strong cheeses	Chocolate cake
Smoked sausage, ham, medium soft cheeses (e.g. Edam)	Islay single malt whisky

BEER AND FOOD PAIRING

BEER STYLE	SUCH AS
Bock	Einbecker Ur-Bock Dunkel
Doppelbock/Eisbock	Andechs Doppelbock Dunkel
Dubbel/Strong dark ale	Trappistes Rochefort 10
Scotch ale	Traquair House Ale
British-style barley wine/ Old ale	Woodforde's Head Cracker
American-style barley wine	Anchor Old Foghorn
Straight lambic/ Gueuze lambic	Cantillon Lambic Bio
Flemish red ale/Flemish brown ale	Rodenbach Grand Cru
Hefeweizen/Kristal weissbier	Weinhenstephaner Hefeweissbier
Dunkelweizen	Weihenstephaner Hefeweissbier Dunkel
Witbier/Bière blanche/ White beer	Blanche de Namur
Weizenbock	Schneider Aventinus
Kriek/Framboise	Drie Fonteinen Oude Kriek
Coffee beer (stout)	Flying Dog Kujo Imperial Coffee Stout

GOOD WITH	PERFECT WITH
Soft cheeses, roasted pork, game fowl	Wild boar
Crème caramel, bread puddings	Obazda (camembert and butter spread)
Braised meats, soft and pungent cheeses	Chocolate fondue
Sticky toffee pudding, braised lamb	Haggis
Cheddar cheeses, long-braised meats	Stilton cheese
Strong blue cheeses, cigars	Citrus-accented dark chocolate truffles
Tangy cheeses, radishes, salads	Roast turkey
Game meats, medium to strong cheeses	Rustic country pâté
Egg dishes, lightly-flavoured fish, salads	Weisswurst (German veal sausage)
Mild curries, falafel, roasted fowl	Charcoal grilled pork
Mussels, goat and other light cheeses	Fluffy cheese omelette
Beef with hoisin sauce, apple pie	Spice cake
Fruit cheesecake, fruit salads	Duck confit
Cookies, chocolate cake, dark chocolates	Late morning and a plate of pastries

BEER AND FOOD PAIRING

IF YOU ARE EATING...	THEN CONSIDER DRINKING...
From a brunch buffet	Hefeweizen, Belgian-style wheat beer, oatmeal stout, standard bitter
A late morning snack	Mild ale, Belgian-style wheat beer, helles, kölsch
A light lunch	Traditional pale ale, mild ale, altbier, dunkelweizen, gose
Assorted charcuterie	Steam beer, best bitter, brown ale, amber ale
From a salad bar	Belgian-style wheat beer, gueuze, kriek, framboise, fruited ale
From a tray of assorted sandwiches	Czech- or German-style pilsner, kölsch, saison
At a barbecue picnic	Traditional or American-style pale ale, brown ale, porter
At a pizza party	Dunkel lager, Vienna lager, American-style pale ale or IPA
Southern US barbecue	American-style pale ale or IPA, steam beer, hoppy brown ale
Bavarian beer hall fare	Märzen, helles, dunkel, hefeweizen, bock, kölsch
Canapés at a cocktail party	German-style pilsner, gueuze, wheat ale, kristal weissbier
Assorted deep-fried appetizers at a bar	Traditional or American-style pale ale, traditional or American style IPA
Vegetables and dip	Vienna lager, saison, Belgian-style enkel, Belgian-style tripel
Salty snacks in front of the television	Czech- or German-style pilsner, traditional or American-style pale ale

IF YOU ARE EATING...	THEN CONSIDER DRINKING...
Spanish tapas	London porter, strong dark ale, bock, Belgian-style spiced ale
Mediterranean mezzes	Golden bitter, Vienna lager, gueuze, weizenbock
Chilled seafood tower	Kölsch, dry stout, porter, Belgian-style wheat beer
Slow-cooker stew	London porter, Dubbel, Strong dark ale, Flemish brown ale
Sunday roast	Traditional IPA, Scottish-style ale, brown ale, ESB
Sushi dinner	Kölsch, cream ale, Belgian-style wheat beer, gose
Thai take out	Saison, traditional pale ale, Belgian-style tripel, bière de garde
Cajun seafood boil	German-style pilsner, American-style pale ale or IPA, dry stout
At a steak house	London porter, porter, brown ale, Scotch ale
With a group at an Indian restaurant	Saison, traditional IPA, American-style pale ale, German-style pilsner
Cake and ice cream	Baltic porter, Scotch ale, doppelbock, old ale
Assorted patisserie	Belgian-style spiced ale (blonde), eisbock, coffee beer, weizenbock
Cheese platter	Best bitter, ESB, British-style barley wine, oatmeal stout
Assorted chocolate truffles	Strong dark ale, double IPA, British-style barley wine, fruited ale

100 GREAT BEER & FOOD DESTINATIONS

UNITED STATES

Monk's Café, 264 South 16th Street, Philadelphia, Pennsylvania

Gramercy Tavern, 42 East 20th Street, New York City, New York

Cochon, 930 Tchoupitoulas Street, New Orleans, Louisiana

Meddlesome Moth, 1621 Oak Lawn Avenue, Dallas, Texas

Ebenezer's Pub, 44 Allen Road, Lovell, Maine

Eastern Standard, 528 Commonwealth Avenue, Boston, Massachusetts

The Monk's Kettle, 3141 16th Street, San Francisco, California

Father's Office, 1018 Montana Avenue, Santa Monica, California

Higgins Restaurant, 1239 SW Broadway, Portland, Oregon

Toronado Seattle, 1205 NE 65th Street, Seattle, Washington

Leon's Full Service, 131 E Ponce de Leon Avenue, Decatur, Georgia

Hopleaf, 5148 N Clark Street, Chicago, Illinois

Euclid Hall, 1317 14th Street, Denver, Colorado

Blue Nile, 2027 Franklin Ave. East, Minneapolis, Minnesota

Farmhouse Tap & Grill, 160 Bank Street, Burlington, Vermont

Birch & Barley, 1337 14th Street NW, Washington D.C.

Three Three Five, 335 North Broadway, Green Bay, Wisconsin

Public House, 3355 Las Vegas Blvd South (in The Venetian), Las Vegas, Nevada

Rhubarb, 7 SW Pack Square, Asheville, North Carolina

Michael's Genuine Food & Drink, 130 NE 40th Street, Miami, Florida

CANADA

beerbistro, 18 King Street East, Toronto, Ontario

Au Pied de Cochon, 536 Avenue Duluth East, Montréal, Québec

Chambar, 568 Beatty Street, Vancouver, British Colombia

Bar Stillwell, 1672 Barrington Street, Halifax, Nova Scotia

Le Select Bistro, 432 Wellington Street West, Toronto

LATIN AMERICA

Mocotó, Avenida Nossa Senhora do Loreto, 1100 - Vila Medeiros, São Paulo, Brazil

Aconchego Carioca, Alameda Jaú, 1372 - Jardim Paulista, São Paulo, Brazil

Pujol, 254 Francisco Petrarca, Mexico City, Mexico

Product C, Avenida Escazu, Escazu San Jose, Costa Rica

Zapata Resto Bar, 2492 Avenida Hernan Cortes, Santiago, Chile

UNITED KINGDOM

White Horse on Parson's Green, 1-3 Parson's Green, London, England

The Bull, 13 North Hill, Highgate, London, England

The Anchor, Main Street, Walberswick, Suffolk, England

The Anderson, Union Street, Fortrose, Scotland

The Oast House, The Avenue Courtyard, Crown Square, Manchester, England

The Olive Branch, Main Street, Clipsham, Rutland, England

The Scran & Scallie, 1 Comely Bank Road, Stockbridge, Edinburgh, Scotland

The Feathered Nest, Nether Westcote, Oxfordshire, England

The Felin Fach Griffin, Felin Fach, Brecon, Wales

Ox and Finch, 920 Sauchiehall Street, Glasgow, Scotland

The Rutland Arms, 86 Brown Street, Sheffield, England

The Belgian Monk, 7 Pottergate, Norwich, England

Le Gavroche, 43 Upper Brook Street, London, England

Bunch of Grapes, Ynysangharad Road, Pontypridd, Wales

The Cross Keys, 107 Water Lane, Leeds, England

Dawsons Restaurant & Bar, Castle Hotel, High Street, Conwy, Wales

Musa Art & Music Café, 33 Exchange Street, Aberdeen, Scotland

AUSTRIA

Friesacher Einkehr, 6 Brunngasse, Anif, Salzburg

BELGIUM

Restobières, 20 Rue Emile Wauters, Brussels

't Hommelhof, 17 Watouplein, Watou

Dock's Café, 7 Jordaenskaai, Antwerp

Botteltje, 19 Louisastraat, Ostend

Bierbrasserie Cambrinus, 19 Philipstockstraat, Bruges
Pichet du Père Marlet, 48 Rue Marcel Lespagne, Hastière
Nuetnigenough, Rue du Lombard, Brussels

CZECH REPUBLIC
Nota Bene, 4 Mikovcova, Prague
Maso & Kobliha, 23 Petrská, Prague

FRANCE
Graindorge, 15 rue de l'Arc de Triomphe, Paris
Qui Plume la Lune, 50 rue Amelot, Paris
Restaurant Le Bloempot, 22 rue des Bouchers, Lille
Le Café Sillon, 46 avenue Jean-Jaurès, Lyon
Le Palégrié, 8 rue du Palais Grillet, Lyon

GERMANY
Altes Mädchen, 28b Lagerstraße, Hamburg
Andechs Monastery, Bergstraße 2, Andech
Das Meisterstück, Hausvogteiplatz 3-4, Berlin
Red Hot, 89 Amalienstrasse, Munich

ISRAEL
Bardak, 38 Keren Hayesod Street, Jerusalem

ITALY
Bir & Fud, 23 via Benedetta, Rome
Ora d'Aria, 11R via dei Georgofili, Florence
La Ratera, 22 via Luigi Ratti, Milan
Osteria a Priori, 39 via dei Priori, Perugia
La Taberna, 49 Vicolo Del Duomo, Palestrina
Lambiczoon, 46 via Friuli, Milan

JAPAN
Wachi, 4F 571 Obiyacho, Nakagyo-ku, Kyoto
Bakushuan, Yoshimatsu Bldg. 2F, 2-27-1 Kita-Otsuka, Toshima-ku, Tokyo
Nawlins, 1-8 Odakicho, Yokosuka, Kanagawa

NETHERLANDS
Dégust, 38 Hoofdstraat, Hoogeveen
Dwars, 24 Egelantiersstraat, Amsterdam
Lieve, 88 Herengracht, Amsterdam
ONS, 41 Walstraat, Enschede

SCANDINAVIA
Den Tatoverede Enke, Baron Boltens Gaard, Gothersgade 8, Copenhagen, Denmark
Brewpub, Vestergade 29, Copenhagen, Denmark
Fairbar, Nørre Allé 66, 8000 Århus C., Denmark
Bryggen Tracteursted, Bryggestredet, Bergen, Norway
Akkurat, 18 Hornsgatan, Stockholm, Sweden
Ölrepubliken, 2B Kronhusgatan, Gothenburg, Sweden

SPAIN
BierCaB, 55 Muntaner, Barcelona
Celler Cal Marino, 54 Carrer de Margarit, Barcelona

ASIA
Chinatown Complex (Good Beer Company w/ hawker stall food), Blk 335 Smith Street, Singapore
The Globe, Garley Building, 45-53 Graham Street, Central, Hong Kong, China
Kaiba, 739 Ding Xi Lu, ChangNing. Shanghai, China

AUSTRALIA
Statler & Waldorf, 25 Caxton Street, Brisbane
Rag & Famish Hotel, 199 Miller Street, North Sydney
The Alliance Hotel, 320 Boundary Street, Brisbane
Cammeray Craft, 504 Miller Street, Cammeray
Tani Eat & Drink, 100 Gavan Street, Bright, Victoria
Merricote, 81 High Street, Melbourne

NEW ZEALAND
The Hop Garden, 13 Pirie Street, Mt. Victoria, Wellington
Pomeroy's Old Brewery Inn, 292 Kilmore Street, Christchurch
Depot Eatery & Oyster Bar, 86 Federal Street, Auckland

Hop-aged Cheddar and Tomato
Grilled Cheese Sandwich 147
hot dogs *90*

I
ice cream 93, *93, 99,* 116
India pale ale (IPA) 22, 26, 28, 64, 80,
99, 100, 108, 122
American-style 28, 116
Belgian 28
Black 28
double or imperial 28, 116
glassware 118
lightly hopped 173
Red 28
sesson 28
and spicy foods 135
traditional 28, 119
Triple 28
White 28
inns, arrival of 12–13
internationalization of beer cuisine
122–123, *122*
Isacsson, Stene 87, *87*

J
Jackson, Michael 75, 186
Michael Jackson's Beer Companion
83
The World Guide to Beer 26
jams 112
Japanese cuisine 127
Japanese izakaya 75, *75,* 76

K
kale: Rösti Potato with Wilted Kale,
Goat Cheese and Beer Beurre
Blanc 188–189
Kennedy, Jim 152
kilning 20
Kitchen Brewery 23
kölsch *see under* golden ale

L
La Ratera restaurant, Milan 166
lagers 20, 72, 87, 100, 115, 124, *124*
carbonated 73
dry 75, *75*
dryly bitter 31
Imperial pale 31
light 72, 75
see also dark lager; pale lager
lamb 107, 108, 114
Lamb Shanks Braised in Porter
with Fresh Thyme 185
Tagine of Lamb 182
lambic beers 23, 26, 48, 112, 114, 119,
166
gueuze lambic 48, 69, 107, 177, 186
straight lambic 48
sweetened gueze 48
lupulin 22

M
McGee, Harold: *On Food and Cooking*
107
McMillan, David 161, *161,* 162, 165
Maillard reaction 99
main dishes 111, *111*
malt beers 69, *69,* 108
see also smoked malt beers; strong
and richly malty beers
malt syrups 161
marinades 107, *107,* 111, *111,* 144
märzen 26, 34
Meddlesome Moth restaurant,
Dallas, Texas 161, *161*

Mercurio, Paul 156, *156,* 158, 194
Cooking with Beer 156
microbreweries 80
mild ale 35, 107, 119, 186
Imperial mild 35
milk stout: Roasted Pumpkin and
Stout Grits 165
Miller, Neil 181
Miller Lite 72
mixed fermentation beers 26, 49, 55,
57, 112, 114
Morin, Brian 111, 135
moules marinières 69, *84*
Munich Oktoberfest festival *67*
mussels 108
Mussels in Coconut and Beer
158–159
mustard 112, *112*
Beer Mustard *135,* 137

N
nachos 73, 94, *94,* 124
New World mixed fermentation 49
New Zealand/Aotearoa pilsner and
pale ale 59
North American-style wheat beer 53
wheat ale 23, 53

O
Oakes, Josh 124, *124*
oatmeal stouts 23, 40
oily foods 94, 97
old ale *see under* barley wine/old ale
Ort, David: *Canadian Craft Beer
Cookbook* 114
Ou, Joon 127, *127,* 128
oud bruin 36
Oxford Companion to Food 64
Oxtail and Pearl Bearley Soup *138,*
141
oysters 65, 90, *122*

P
pairing and context 93, *93*
pale ale 22, 28, 64, 90, 107, 108, 116,
119, 122, 123, *123, 124,* 132
golden 173
pale and not-too-bitter beers 32–34
pale lager 34, 69, 124
helles 34, 66, 67, 75, 90, 99, 107, 119,
122–123, 189
märzen/Oktoberfestbier 34, 66
Vienna lager 34, 104, *104,* 108, 128
paring and context 93, *93*
Passerelli, Eduardo 148, *148,* 151
pasta 90, 108, 166
Paxton, Sean 111, 138, *138,* 141
pie fillings 116
pilsner 19, 31, 66, 69, 87, 90, 99, *104,*
119, 122, 156
Czech- or Bohemian-style 31, 71, *71*
German-style 31
global-style 31
Imperial 31
New Zealand/Aotearoa pilsner and
pale ale 59
pizzas 76, *76,* 97, 124
ploughman's lunch 186
pork 66–67, *67,* 76, 89, 90, 97, *97,* 166,
186
Beer Braised Pork Belly with a
Creole Seasoning 142
pork pies *104, 112,* 186
Pork Ribs with Beer and Chocolate
151
porter 64, 87, 90, 107, 114, *122*
see also stout/porter

potatoes: Rösti Potato with Wilted
Kale, Goat Cheese and Beer Beurre
Blanc 188–189
pretzels 94
Princess Louise, Holborn, London *62*
prunes 135
Prune and Chocolate Brownies 191
puddings *99,* 116
pumpkin: Roasted Pumpkin and
Stout Grits 165
pumpkin beer 58–59
Purity Brewing Co., Warwickshire *19*

Q
quadrupel *see under* abbey-style
strong dark ale
Quilon restaurant, London 100, *100*

R
rabbit 69, 107
ratebeer.com 93
Reinheitsgebot (Bavarian purity law)
16, 23
relishes 112
Restobières, Brussels, Belgium 177,
177
Rinaldi, Marco 166
Rogue Ales 23
rye pale ale/rye P.A. 23, 59

S
Saint Tavern, Toronto, Canada 135,
135
saisons 30, 119, 132, 156, 161, 188
salad dressings 112
salmon: Hop 'Hot Smoked' Salmon &
Beer Hollandaise 173
salty foods 73, 94
Samichlaus 6
Sandwich, Hop-aged Cheddar and
Tomato Grilled Cheese 147
saucing 108
Saunders, Lucy 111, 144, *144,* 147, 192
Cooking with Beer 144, *144*
Dinner in the Beer Garden 124
sausage rolls 186
sausages 65, 89, 135, 177
scallops: Bay Scallops with Sweet
Corn & Barley Wine Tapioca 162
Schlabs, Keith 161
Schneider, Georg 96
schwarzbier *see under* dark lager
Scotch ale 46, 99, *99,* 108, 119, 144, 151,
182, 185
peated Scotch ale 46
seafood 108, 123
"session beers" 186
shrimp marinade 107
Slosberg, Peter 116
smoked beers 42–43, 87
grodziskie/grätzer 42
peated malt beer 42
rauchbier 39, 42, 66, 148
smoked porter/stout 42
see also malt beers
soups 90, *115,* 123
Oxtail and Pearl Bearley Soup *138,*
141
speciality malts 20
spiced ale 165
Belgian-style spiced ale 55, 99, *99,*
119
New World spiced beer 55
pumpkin ale 174
sahti 55
spiced beers 23, 54–55, 69
spicy foods 73, 94, 97, 100, 135

steak and ale pie 76
steak and kidney pie 65
steaming 108
Steenson, Warren 152
steins *67*
stewing 108
stews 69, 90, 108, *108*
stir fries *123*
Stone Brewing Co. *16*
storing beer 119, *119*
Stout Brown Sauce 136
stout/porter 20, 23, 40–41, 65, 90, *112,*
116, 119, 156, 173
Baltic porter 40, 192
dry stout/Irish style stout 40
hoppy porter 28
Imperial stout 40, 99, 186, 192, 195
London porter 40
oatmeal stout 23, 40
porter 40
stout astringency 138
Stout-steamed Edamame 131
sweet stout 107
White Stout 40
strong and richly malty beers 44–47
Sumerians 12
svetlý 71
Swedish beer 87
sweetness factor 99, *99*

T
tart, spontaneous or mixed
fermentation beers 48–50
Trappist ales 69, 93, *93,* 118, *118*
tripel *see under* golden ale
turkey 107

V
Vallins, Jesse 135, *135,* 136, 137
veal 138
venison 107
vinegar 112
Visser, Margaret: *The Rituals of
Dinner* 10
Voodoo Doughnut chain 23

W
water 18–19, *19*
waterzooi 69, 177
weissbier *see under* German-style
wheat beer
weizenbock *see* German-style
weizenbock
'wet hop' beers 22
wheat ales 119
wheat beers 23, 75, 100, 107, 166
Belgian style 107, 132, 155, 158, 168
refreshing and light-bodied 51–53
wheat wines 23, 46
White Horse gastropub, Parson's
Green, London 186
wildcard beers 58–59
wines 10, 94, 100, 138
witbier *see under* Belgian-style wheat
beer
wort 16, 22

Y
yeast 20–21, *20*

PICTURE CREDITS

Special Photography
Many thanks to Peter Cassidy for recipe photography in the Beer Cuisine section, Emily Kydd for food styling and Iris Bromet for sourcing props.

Beer and Food Matching Charts: Beer bottle photography by Peter Cassidy.

Picture research: Emily Hedges

The publisher would like to thank the following sources for their kind permission to reproduce the images in this book.

Back jacket credits: left Stone Brewing Co.; centre Beer Lens; right CRATE Brewery.

Page 2 Beer Lens; 6 Beer Lens; 7 BrewDog; 8 Beer Lens; 11 top The Craft Beer Co.; 11 bottom Beer Lens; 12 © Corbis/Bettmann; 13 Private Collection/Photo © Christie's Images/Bridgeman Images; 14 Simon Murrell for Jacqui Small; 16 The Craft Beer Co.; 17 BrewDog; 18 Shutterstock.com/Dominique de La Croix; 20 top Shutterstock.com/Eugenia Lucasenco; 20 bottom Shutterstock.com/Dave M Hunt; 21 Shutterstock.com/saiko3p; 22 Shutterstock.com/Jan Faulkner; 23 Shutterstock.com/Best Photo Studio; 24 CRATE Brewery; 27 Beer Lens; 60 Liszt Collection/Heritage Images/Getty Images; 62 Beer Lens; 63 SSPL/Getty Images; 64 The Craft Beer Co.; 65 Beer Lens; 66 Munchen Tourismus/Foto Werner Boehm; 67 left Munchen Tourismus/Foto Frank Bauer; 67 right Bayern Tourismus; 68 top Shutterstock.com/Natalia Lisovskaya; 68 bottom left Beer Lens; 68 bottom right Shutterstock.com/Dubassy; 70 left U Fleku; 70 right Simon Murrell for Jacqui Small; 72 Beer Lens; 73 left Shutterstock.com/Joshua Resnick; 73 right The Craft Beer Co.; 74 top and bottom Shutterstock.com/twoKim; 75 Shutterstock.com/Aaron Choi; 77 CRATE Brewery; 78 BrewDog; 81 top Beer Lens; 81 bottom The Craft Beer Co.; 82 top Beer Lens, 83 Beer Lens; 84 Shutterstock.com/oldbunyip; 86 photo of Steen Isacsson/Patrik Lindqvist; 88 photo courtesy of Fuller's; 89 Shutterstock.com/Maxim Kostenko; 91 BrewDog; 92 top Beer Lens ; 92 bottom photo courtesy of Fuller's; 95 top Shutterstock.com; 95 bottom left and right John Carey for Jacqui Small; 96 top and bottom left Schneider-Weisse; 96 bottom right photo courtesy Susanne Hecht; 98 top The Craft Brewing Co.; 98 bottom Shutterstock.com/Margoe Edwards; 99 Photo courtesy of Fuller's; 101 photo courtesy of Sriram Aylur; 102 CRATE Brewery/Matt Russell; 104 The Craft Beer Co.; 105 and 106 Stone Brewing Co.; 109 Shutterstock.com; 110 U Fleku; 111 left Shutterstock.com; 111 right Thornbridge Brewery; 113 top photo courtesy of Fuller's; 113 bottom Beer Lens; 114 Shutterstock.com; 115 Shutterstock.com/Brent Hofacker; 117 top left Thornbridge Brewery; 117 top right Shutterstock.com/Liliya Kandrashevich; 117 bottom Shutterstock.com/Letterberry; 118 Beer Lens; 120 Shutterstock.com/Freeskyline; 122 Shutterstock.com/Natalia Lisovskaya; 123 Stone Brewing Co.; 125 top image courtesy of Josh Oakes; 125 bottom John Carey for Jacqui Small; 126 top and bottom ©Fumiaki Yamazaki; 133 image courtesy of Daniel Goh; 134 top and bottom photos courtesy of Jesse Vallins; 139 and 140 photos courtesy of Sean Paxton; 145 top left photo courtesy of Lucy Saunders; 145 top right Shutterstock.com; 145 bottom Shutterstock.com/Stockcreations; 149 photo courtesy of Eduardo Passerelli; 153 John Valls; 157 top and bottom photos courtesy of Paul Mercurio; 160 photo courtesy of David McMillan; 167 photo courtesy of Salvatore Garofalo; 171 photos courtesy of Mitch Adams; 176 CityPlug.com/Elliott Laub; 180 photo courtesy of Martin Bosley; 187 top photo courtesy of Mark Dorber/Sarah Groves; 187 bottom photo courtesy of Mark Dorber/Roy Strutt Photography; 196 The Craft Beer Co.; 198 above Almond & Coconut Pancakes with Roasted Spiced Plums from Gut Gastronomy by Vicki Edgson & Adam Palmer, photography by Lisa Linder; 198 below Sonhos from World's Best Cakes by Roger Pizey, photography by Sarka Babicka; 200 above A Simple Goat's Cheese Salad from A Country Cook's Kitchen by Alison Walker, photography by Tara Fisher; 200 centre Blu di Langa, below Baked Vacherin from Cheese by Patricia Michelson, photography by Lisa Linder; 202 above Smoked Salmon with Goat's Cheese Salad and Mead Dressing, below Sea Bass with Roasted Vegetables and Butter Bean Sauce from Fitness Gourmet by Christian Coates, photography by Yuki Sugiura; 204 above Tagliatelle with Asparagus, Almonds and Mint from Love Italian Food by Maddalena Caruso and Stefano Scatà, photography by Stefano Scatà; 204 below Cold Sesame Noodles from Asian Cook by Terry Tan, photography by Michael Paul; 206 above Texas Porterhouse Steak with Spicy Chilli Salsa and Onion Rings from Steak by Paul Gayler, photography by Peter Cassidy; 206 centre Bloody Mary Burger from Burgers by Paul Gayler, photography by Gus Filgate; 206 below Wild Boar Sausages with Fennel-braised Potatoes and Tomato Chermoula from Sausages by Paul Gayler, photography by Will Heap; 208 above Porcini, Hazelnut, Thyme and Garlic Butter from Chicken & Other Birds by Kevin Summers; 208 below Murgh makhna from Chicken & Other Birds by Paul Gayler, photography by Kevin Summers; 210 above Masala Roasted Root Vegetables from Honestly Healthy for Life by Natasha Corrett & Vicki Edgson, photography by Lisa Linder; 210 centre Chickpea and Sweet Potato Stew from Honestly Healthy by Natasha Corrett & Vicki Edgson, Lisa Linder; 210 below Vanilla Cheesecake from World's Best Cakes by Roger Pizey, photography by Sarka Babicka; 213 above Individual Game Pies from A Country Cook's Kitchen by Alison Walker, photography by Tara Fisher; 213 centre Hearty Dutch Breakfast Board from Cheese by Patricia Michelson, photography by Lisa Linder; 213 below Whole Roasted Poussins with Lemon and Herb Purée from Chicken & Other Birds by Paul Gayler, photography by Kevin Summers; 215 above Taglierini with Kale and Hot Sausage Sauce from Sausages by Paul Gayler, photography by Will Heap; 215 centre Flash-fried Black Pudding with Sage-cream Cabbage and Apple Chutney from Sausages by Paul Gayler, photography by Will Heap; 215 below Rosticini with Polenta and Aubergine Balsamic Vine Tomatoes from Sausages by Paul Gayler, photography by Will Heap; 216 above Chicken Casserole with Orange Blossom Honey, Tomato and Chickpeas from Chicken & Other Birds by Paul Gayler, photography by Kevin Summers; 216 centre Creamy Chicken Liver Pate from A Country Cook's Kitchen by Alison Walker, photography by Tara Fisher; 216 below Devil's Food Cake from World's Best Cakes by Roger Pizey, photography by Sarka Babicka

PUBLISHER'S ACKNOWLEDGEMENTS
The publisher wishes to thank the many breweries from around the world that kindly provided images of their beers, beer labels, bars, food and breweries reproduced here.

Grateful thanks to the following online retailers, beer shops and breweries for advice and supply of beers and food for photography:

Ales by Mail www.alesbymail.com
Anspach & Hobday, 118 Druid Street, Bermondsey, London SE1 2HH www.anspachandhobday.com
Beer Ritz, www.beerritz.co.uk
Beer Shop, St Albans, 71 London Rd, St Albans, Hertfordshire AL1 1LN www.beershopstalbans.com
Beers of Europe, www.beersofeurope.co.uk
Fuller's Brewery, The Griffin Brewery, Chiswick Lane South, London W4 2QB www.fullers.co.uk
Kris Wines, 394 York Way, London N7 9LW, www.kriswines.com
Thornbridge Brewery, Riverside Brewery, Buxton Road, Bakewell, Derbyshire, DE45 1GS www.thornbridgebrewery.co.uk

AUTHOR'S ACKNOWLEDGEMENTS
There is no way in the world that I could possibly list here all the individuals who have contributed to my personal explorations of beer and food through the decades, from chefs and enthusiastic eaters to brewers, publicans and restaurateurs, butchers, cheese mongers and other purveyors of fine foods, and countless friends across the dinner table. Many are profiled in these pages and some are sadly no longer with us, including my original culinary influence, my mother Jean Beaumont, and the man who was in many ways a mentor as well as a friend, Michael Jackson.

To the rest, to all of you out there who have shared your thoughts and your recipes, a glass of beer, a hastily enjoyed snack or a gourmet meal, I offer my sincere thanks and appreciation. Let's do it all again sometime soon!

On a more practical level, I'd like to thank my editor Jo Copestick and everyone at Jacqui Small who helped this book along, my agent Clare Pelino and all my friends in Toronto and beyond who endured months of my bellyaching as I worked to complete this book on schedule. Special thanks to Rob, Jim, Matt and everyone at Bar Hop, who provided a sanctuary up the road for when the pressures grew a bit overwhelming, and Jean-Jacques, Frédéric and the wonderful staff at Le Select Bistro, for the oasis of calm that is Toronto's finest French restaurant.

Most of all, thank you to my lovely, insightful and incredibly tolerant wife, Maggie. I never would have made it this far without you, sweetheart.